Praise for

Lost in Suburbia

"Reading *Lost in Suburbia*, locked in my bathroom all alone, I laughed, I cried (from laughing), and then I laughed some more. When you're feeling overwhelmed by the maddening, mind-numbing demands of motherhood, get 'lost in suburbia.' You'll be so glad you did."

—Jenna McCarthy, author of *If It Was Easy,
They'd Call the Whole Damn Thing a Honeymoon* and *The Parent Trip*

"*Lost in Suburbia* had me snorting with laughter throughout. It's painfully relatable and simply hilarious. If you've ever looked at your suburban life with kids and wondered how the hell you got there, this book is for you."

—Jill Smokler, *New York Times* bestselling author of
Confessions of a Scary Mommy

"I love this woman."

—Jenny Lawson, aka The Bloggess, author of
New York Times bestseller *Let's Pretend This Never Happened*

"Beckerman's effervescent, irreverent humor is peppered with heartfelt poignancy in this most relatable memoir about motherhood and rediscovering your bad-mom self."

—Jenny Gardiner, author of the Kindle bestsellers
Slim to None and *Sleeping with Ward Cleaver*

"*Lost in Suburbia* is packed with the funniest truths and palmetto bug fears. When you put it down to drive the carpool, you'll miss your new best friend."

—Gwendolen Gross, author of *When She Was Gone* and
the bestselling novel *The Orphan Sister*

"Beckerman is the girlfriend you wish you had when you were expecting and the cool mom you stalk at Mommy and Me. Her stories of new motherhood are completely relatable, funny, and heart wrenching."

—Lela Davidson, author of
Blacklisted from the PTA and *Who Peed on My Yoga Mat?*

continued . . .

Lost in Suburbia

How I Got Pregnant,
Lost Myself,
and Got My Cool Back
in the New Jersey Suburbs

Tracy Beckerman

A Perigee Book

A PERIGEE BOOK
Published by the Penguin Group
Penguin Group (USA) Inc.
375 Hudson Street, New York, New York 10014, USA

USA / Canada / UK / Ireland / Australia / New Zealand / India / South Africa / China

Penguin Books Ltd., Registered Offices: 80 Strand, London WC2R 0RL, England
For more information about the Penguin Group, visit penguin.com.

Library of Congress Cataloging-in-Publication Data

Beckerman, Tracy.
Lost in suburbia : how I got pregnant, lost myself, and got my cool back in the
New Jersey suburbs / Tracy Beckerman.— First edition.
pages   cm
ISBN 978-0-399-15993-0
1. Beckerman, Tracy.   2. Mothers—New Jersey—Biography.
3. Motherhood—New Jersey—Humor.   4. Suburban life—New Jersey—Humor.   I. Title.
HQ759.B275A3 2013
306.874'309749—dc23   2012043699

First edition: April 2013

PRINTED IN THE UNITED STATES OF AMERICA

10   9   8   7   6   5   4   3   2   1

Text design by Laura K. Corless

This book describes the real experiences of real people. The author has disguised the identities
of some, and in some instances created composite characters, but none of these changes has
affected the truthfulness and accuracy of her story. Penguin is committed to publishing works
of quality and integrity. In that spirit, we are proud to offer this book to our readers;
however, the story, the experiences, and the words are the author's alone.

While the author has made every effort to provide accurate telephone numbers, Internet
addresses, and other contact information at the time of publication, neither the publisher nor
the author assumes any responsibility for errors, or for changes that occur after publication.
Further, the publisher does not have any control over and does not assume any
responsibility for author or third-party websites or their content.

Most Perigee books are available at special quantity discounts for bulk purchases for sales
promotions, premiums, fund-raising, or educational use. Special books, or book excerpts,
can also be created to fit specific needs. For details, write: Special Markets,
Penguin Group (USA) Inc., 375 Hudson Street, New York, New York 10014.

For Mom and Dad
who love me all the way up to the sky

Author's Note

This "momoir" is considered nonfiction and I have done my best to re-create the events in this story to the best of my memory without the slightest embellishment or enhancement of the events or conversations that took place. And if you believe that, then clearly you have never read my humor column.

Additionally, all the people in this story are real, although most of the names have been changed and many of the characters have been combined to keep me out of trouble. If you recognize yourself in here, it's probably not you, unless you were mean to me, and then it probably is you. That's called payback, baby!

Thanks for playing.

Contents

Part Two

Prologue

"*Good morning, ma'am.*"

"*Good morning, Officer.*"

"*Are you aware that you made an illegal left turn onto this street?*"

"*No, sir,*" I lied.

"*Didn't you see the sign at the corner that said, 'No left turn'?*" he asked in standard police monotone.

"*What sign, Officer?*" I responded in standard suburban-ite bull doody.

"*That big sign over there, Mommy!*" shouted by daughter from the backseat, as she pointed back in the direction of the school. Apparently, my almost three-year-old, who could not yet read, was an idiot savant when it came to interpreting street signs.

"I guess I missed that sign." I shrugged. "There were too many minivans blocking my view."

He gave me a dubious look and then lowered his oversized mirrored Ray-Bans. If I hadn't been dressed in my bathrobe, I might have actually made a snarky comment about his '80s-style sunglasses. But people who live in fluffy, blue bathrobes shouldn't throw stones.

"Is that your bathrobe?" he asked suspiciously, peering down at my robe. The cat was out of the bag.

"Yes, it is, Officer."

"And are those birds on your bathrobe?" he wondered.

"That's Mommy's ducky bathrobe," chimed in my daughter from the backseat. "She likes it 'cuz it quacks her up!!" She quipped, quoting a bad family joke. The cop wasn't amused.

"Can I see your license and registration, please?" he finally asked.

"Hey, Mama. Hey, Mommy. Hey, Mom," chanted my daughter.

"One minute, puss," I said as I rummaged through my handbag, which was equipped for every possible kid emergency from a hunger meltdown to a snot explosion, but apparently not for being stopped by a cop.

"Hey, Mama. Hey, Mommy. Mamamamamamamama . . ." she repeated.

"Your mommy is busy right now," said the officer impatiently.

"Hmmph!" snorted my daughter. "I wasn't talking to you, you big bubba!"

I gave the cop a withering smile. I was going to jail for a very long time.

In my bathrobe.

Part One

One day Alice came to a fork in the robe and saw a Cheshire cat in a tree. "Which robe do I take?" she asked. "Where do you want to go?" was his response. "I don't know," Alice answered. "Then," said the cat, "it doesn't matter."

—Not quite Lewis Carroll,
Alice's Adventures in Wonderland

Chapter 1

I'm Not Fat, I'm Just Pregnant.
Okay, I'm Fat, Too

I know I had been cool once . . .

I don't remember all that clearly what made me so cool except I have this vague recollection of wearing a lot of black, drinking a fair amount of scotch, and being single. Of course, that could describe almost anyone attending an Irish wake, so maybe those are not good indicators of what makes someone cool.

In my case, though, I think there were a number of contributing factors:

1. I Lived in New York City

The real New York City, as in *Manhattan*. When I first met my husband, he said he lived in New York City, too, which I thought bode well for his status as my future husband. But when I asked him where, exactly, in New York City, he said, "Brooklyn."

"Brooklyn isn't the *city*," I replied haughtily. "It's a *buhhh-rough*." That could have been the end of the relationship right there, and I never would have married him, had his children, and gotten stretch marks. But he had cute eyes and a crooked smile that made me melt so I decided to overlook the fact that he had severe geographic dementia.

Unfortunately, living in New York City on a salary that was somewhere between the national poverty line and what a migrant coffee-bean picker in South America makes was not as glamorous as they make it out to be on *Sex and the City*. Before I met my husband, I shared a dumpy one-bedroom apartment with a girlfriend from high school. Actually, my friend and I shared the bedroom but the cockroaches had the lease on the rest of the place. In an effort to rid the place of the roaches, I finally went out and got this "industrial strength, works even in the Amazon, one spritz and they're definitely dead" bug spray. The next time I saw one, I sprayed. Not only didn't it die, it actually sprouted wings and flew at me.

In a panic I called home. My mother told me that if it flies, it isn't a cockroach . . . it's a palmetto bug. I told her that nomenclature was not really the issue when it concerned a five-inch-tall insect that had taken up residence in my living room.

She said, live and let live.

I said, fine, let it live in your house.

She said, if I met a nice Jewish guy and got married I wouldn't have to live in a dump with giant flying bugs.

She was right about that part, anyway.

2. I Worked in Television

This sounds a lot cooler than it actually was, except for the time I loaned Charlotte Rae my black bra for her appearance on a TV show I was working on because she was wearing a white bra under a black shirt and you could see it on camera. I'm not sure if I truly was the only one working on the show who wore the same size bra as Charlotte Rae or if this was my humiliating rite of passage into the glamorous world of television production, but the end result was the same. Of course, even this sounds cooler than it actually was because (a) almost no one knows who Charlotte Rae is anymore, (b) no one watched the TV show I worked on, and (c) I had to walk around for half a day holding up my boobs with my elbows and occasionally one would break free and swing precariously toward the cameras and boom mics, disrupting the taping.

Yes, they were that big.

Eventually I worked my way out of entertainment TV and into a career in TV news promotion. The main difference here was that in entertainment TV, you know they are making stuff up. In TV news, you're never sure what's real and what's not.

3. I Got Expensive Haircuts

My husband used to get his hair cut at a place in Greenwich Village that charged about five dollars a cut. He was very proud of the fact that he got a good haircut for so little money and he would constantly try to convince me to get my hair cut where he did. Of course his definition of a good haircut was somewhat different than mine. My feeling was, if you look like you've been run over by a possessed lawn mower that answers to the name of *Christine*, it's not a particularly good haircut.

As far as I was concerned, the only redeeming quality of my husband's haircuts was his barber. Yuri was an old Russian transplant who didn't cut hair particularly well and didn't say much, but when he did speak, he was very wise. Whenever my husband would complain about me early in our marriage, Yuri would listen quietly and then say, "There is old Russian saying: Happy wife, happy life." These words served my husband well throughout the years. Much better than his haircuts did.

Of course, part of my husband keeping me happy was to keep quiet when I spent the equivalent of a month's salary on my haircuts (which was not as much as you would think considering the aforementioned wages I made). I didn't have a barber. I had a stylist named Romel who was a hotheaded, hot-blooded Arab Israeli who wanted to jump my bones. He had no problem with the fact that he was Arab and I was Jewish and he assured me that not only would he give me the best haircut I ever had but the best sex, too. Since I wasn't interested in him, even in the name of Mideast peace, I politely declined the best sex but flirted just enough to ensure the best haircut. It really was the best haircut I ever had while I lived in the city and I was truly devastated when he got in a fight with the salon owner, the salon mysteriously went up in flames, and Romel coincidentally and suddenly disappeared.

4. I Spent My Lunch Hour at Sample Sales

When I was a cool city chick, I loved great clothes. Unfortunately in my industry, at my salary, I only had enough money to cover rent and roach traps. This meant if I wanted cool clothes, I either had to steal them or had to find great bargains. That's when I discovered sample sales. The problem with sample sales though, is that there are usually no dressing rooms, so if you wanted to try something on, you had to strip down in the middle of the sample sale. I'm sure that one day one of my children will find pictures on the Internet of my naked body that were taken by sleazy sample-sale security camera personnel and the kids will be only slightly less traumatized than when they found the pictures of me giving birth to them.

5. I Could Name All Fifty States in Twelve Seconds
What? You don't think that's cool? Okay, maybe not. But I did live in New York City.

. . .

To reflect on what it is to be cool, and how to get your cool back once you've lost it, it helps to figure out what might have caused you to stop being cool in the first place. For me, it was that little thing called "pregnancy." Had I known that pregnancy was going to so completely undermine all the hard work I had put into my coolness, I might have ordered a baby from a catalog instead and called it a day.

Of course there are things about being pregnant that are cool, like seeing the first sonogram where your baby looks like an alien monkey, and feeling the baby kick, and pretending that Krispy Kreme doughnuts are good for you and the baby. But, it's definitely hard to look cool when you are so big you should have your own zip code. When I was pregnant, it was impossible to hide all that bigness with cute maternity clothes.

This was before Liz Lange designed maternity clothes. This was before even Old Navy had a maternity department. When I was pregnant, I think all maternity clothes were made by Garanimals. All the tops matched the pants and everything was in big bold prints and looked like it had been designed by an eighty-year-old woman named Gertrude who lived in Century Village. There was no black. There were no jeans. There was certainly no leather. Just polyester. Lots and lots of polyester.

The good news is, pregnancy does come to an end eventually. The bad news, however, is that being pregnant and uncool almost always segues into being a new mom and uncool. It's funny how walking around for a year with spit-up, drool, partially digested mashed bananas, and all other forms of baby regurgitation on your clothing will make you very, very uncool.

Needless to say, I was cool with the other moms. Those mashed bananas are like a merit badge of honor. It is the ultimate sign of solidarity in the sorority of motherhood. Unfortunately, it just didn't go with my DKNY tops.

Of course I didn't know any of this the day I peed on a stick and I saw a big plus sign telling me I was pregnant.

I remember sitting my husband down at the teeny, tiny kitchen table in the all-in-one living room/dining room/kitchen/bedroom of our teeny, tiny apartment in New York City. Then I plunked a jar of spaghetti sauce in front of him.

"What's this?" he asked.

I grinned like the proverbial Cheshire cat. "What's it say?"

"Prego."

"Well . . . ?" I smiled knowingly.

"We are . . . having pasta for dinner?" he guessed.

"Try again," I coaxed.

"Chicken Parm?" he wondered.

"Argh!! It's not about food!" I glared at him and wondered whether it was the Y chromosome or the ability to grow facial hair that makes men so dense.

"What. Does. It. Say??" I repeated.

"Prego!" he repeated. He looked at me with exasperation and then shrugged.

"I got nuthin'."

"Prego," I said. "Preggggoooo."

He shook his head.

"I'm *pregnant*!!" I shouted.

"Really?"

"Yes!" I beamed.

"Cool!" He grinned. "But what does that have to do with spaghetti sauce?"

. . .

I really should not have been surprised that I got pregnant so easily. When we made the decision to launch our baby-making efforts, we went away for a romantic weekend to a touristy seaport and checked into a hotel called the Seamen's Inn. What did surprise me was how, almost from the moment of conception, I started to feel really, really lousy and resemble, in the most unattractive way imaginable, the Michelin Man.

This was not exactly the way I had pictured my first pregnancy. For some women, pregnancy is a golden time. They have a real glow about them and they have this cute little belly that makes them look like they just swallowed a basketball. I was not one of those women. When I was pregnant, I had a glow . . . but it was from throwing up all the time. I didn't look like I swallowed a basketball: I looked like I'd swallowed the whole basketball team. And it wasn't just my belly that got fat. My whole body got fat. My butt got fat, my ankles got fat, even my earlobes got fat. I was this big, fat, pukey pregnant woman and I was truly miserable. One day as I was puking and getting fatter, my mother-in-law came to me and said, "I know you feel horrible, but you get this wonderful gift at the end."

"Yeah," I said. "Hemorrhoids."

Clearly it's hard to be cool when you're tossing your cookies all the time and when you're so big you think about hanging a "Caution: Wide Load" sign on your backside as you walk through the supermarket aisles. I was so huge that one night while my husband was on the phone with his brother, our microwave oven started beeping and my brother-in-law asked if that sound was me, backing up.

I was, actually, kind of prepared for the fact that I was going to get bigger. I just didn't think I was going to get bigger all over. And when I say all over, I mean, specifically, my boobs. I was not small to start with—I was a D cup—but by my seventh month of pregnancy, I got to a letter in the alphabet I didn't even know existed for bra sizes. It was a letter most kids don't even get to when they first learn the alphabet song. My boobs were so big, you couldn't even tell I was pregnant until my third trimester because they obscured everything else from the waist down. This was not a fun time for me, and the only one who was really, truly excited about this development, other than the ladies in the bra department at the underwear store, was my husband. He felt like his mammary ship had come in and he had won the boob lottery. Of course, there was no way he could get near the golden orbs with my head in the toilet all the time, but he was happy from afar.

The irony of this breast situation was that I'd been flat as a board until I was fourteen years old. I grew up in the shadow of my mother's 34Ds, and while everyone had assumed I would follow in her bra steps, by high school the general consensus was that I had probably inherited my boobs, or lack thereof, from my father's side of the family. But then the compassionate hand of God reached out the summer of my fifteenth year, slapped me on the back, and out popped a pair of enormous 36D breasts. There was no transition. No awkward development stage. One day I looked like Olive Oyl—the next I was Jessica Rabbit.

Not having been privy to these new developments, my parents called me midway through sleep-away camp to ask what I wanted them to bring me on visiting day.

"I need some bras," I whispered into the office phone. "Big ones!"

Had I known all those nights when I was praying for breasts that God was only just warming up with me and was going to hand me a giant upgrade during pregnancy, I might have prayed for something a little less obtrusive, like a pet elephant.

Meanwhile, back at pregnancy central, the doctor told me that the uber-boobs were growing in preparation for making milk, and the being nauseous part meant that my body was working really hard to give the growing fetus everything it needed. This was the first indication I had that bearing children is actually really bad for your body. I figured anything that makes you throw up all the time, without the benefit of a good drunken binge the night before, is just not something I was interested in. Yet shockingly, with all the vomiting, I still managed to put on sixty pounds with each pregnancy. This made no sense to me. When I was a teenager, we threw up to *lose* weight. Naturally, the doctor was a little miffed that I'd gained so much weight until I explained that I had no idea how it happened and I was only eating the Pop-Tarts and doughnuts to chase away the nausea. The other interesting thing was that I still gained weight despite the fact that I was carrying my son up in my lungs and had a constant case of acute heartburn. This just goes to prove my theory that a hungry pregnant woman will eat anything that isn't nailed down, no matter how nauseous she is, no matter how bad her heartburn is, and no matter how many horror stories her ob-gyn tells about trying to vaginally deliver a twelve-pound baby.

Even if the scale didn't tell me I was the size of a house, I knew it from the looks of strangers. So many people asked me if I was carrying twins or triplets that eventually I decided to just save face and lie.

"My husband and I wanted a lot of kids and I wasn't crazy about getting pregnant, so I decided to get it all over with at once," I would tell them.

"How many?" they would ask.

"Five."

"You're carrying *five* babies?" they would say incredulously.

"Yes, I am!" I would boast. "We actually wanted eight, but thought five would be a more reasonable number." This was years before Kate and her eight and Octomom, and anyone who had five kids at one time was either taking massive fertility drugs or was a beagle. However, this definitely got me off the hook for looking so fat and made those women who looked like they just swallowed a basketball very jealous of my wondrous uterus.

Of course, even the fattest pregnant women know that as

long as you are pregnant, you can blame any amount of weight gain on the baby. But once that baby comes out, it is a completely different story. Naturally, the women who looked like they swallowed a basketball when they were pregnant, looked like they had never been pregnant at all within a week of giving birth, whereas I looked like I was still pregnant for years after my baby was born. I remember pushing my son in his stroller when he was three months old and having a woman stop and ask me when the baby was due.

I looked at her in disbelief and then gestured to the infant in the stroller.

"What do you think this is?" I asked her. "A *salami*?"

I'm sure that I'm the last woman she ever asked *that* question to.

Fortunately, when you're a mom, you get a "Get Out of Fat Jail Free" card for as long as you have young kids. Whenever you feel fat, you can tell someone you still haven't lost "the baby weight," and they will nod in understanding. It's like the Sisterhood of the Traveling Fat Pants. We all wear Fat Pants, otherwise known as Mom Jeans, after the baby is born because they are all we can get over our Baby Bellies. And the Baby Belly, of course, is not the belly you have when you are pregnant; it is the belly you are left with after the baby is born. It is a cross between the wrinkled look of a Shar-Pei and the girth of Jabba the Hutt. Clearly not a good look for anyone, but especially for a new mom who used to have a smokin' hot bod and now looks like her stomach needs to be ironed.

The problem with the baby-belly excuse is that this is an explanation you can legitimately use for years, although the excuse does tend to wear a bit thin by the time your kids are in grad school. Additionally, a lot of us who have more than one kid make the critical mistake of not losing the baby belly *before* we become pregnant with the next baby. I am a pragmatist and it just seemed silly to me to work so hard to lose all the baby weight when I was just going to gain it all back again in a year. Then I had the weight to lose from the first pregnancy *and* the weight to lose from the second pregnancy *plus* the extra weight I gained from being so depressed about all the weight I gained with both kids. There has been a lot of discussion in recent years about postpartum depression and I know that I certainly was depressed after my kids were born. Doctors are quick to blame postpartum depression on raging hormones, but I'm pretty sure that postpartum depression is actually a chemical disruption caused by an overabundance of pregnancy fat cells that migrate into your head and clog up your brain.

Chapter 2

Why You Shouldn't Let Your Mohel Take the Red-Eye to the Bris

Our son decided to make his entrance into the world three weeks early. For some reason he was in a big, fat hurry for about thirty seconds when my water broke, and then must have changed his mind because the ensuing labor lasted thirty-six hours. There is not much I am willing to do for thirty-six hours, the least of which is pant like a dog and writhe in pain every two minutes to push out a baby that really has no interest in being born at that moment in time. My husband was quick to reassure me that most women completely forget the entire labor and delivery process as soon as it is over. I am quick to reassure him that I remember every second of that experience and only a steady stream of expensive gifts throughout my lifetime will help take the edge off those painful memories.

I always found it amusing that you have to spend a year

learning to drive before you can get a license, but all you need to do to become a parent is have sex and forget to use a condom. When my son was born and the nurse handed him to me, I held him for a little while and then handed him back.

"He's crying," I explained.

"Yup. Babies do dat when dey are hungry," she said in a thick island accent, handing him back to me.

"I guess you better feed him then," I responded, passing him back to her like a hot potato.

She laughed a big, hearty, New-York-City-nurse laugh.

"Darlin', I got me some mighty fine breasts, but dey do not have what interests dis here young man," she retorted. She passed the crying infant back to me and opened up her arms like Moses as if to say, "The lord hath given you two mountains from which you shall feedeth your child." I looked down at my monster boobs and realized that it was lunchtime and the special on the menu for today . . . was me. Unfortunately, I didn't have the operating manual and I had no idea how to turn the damn things on. Although my labor had lasted almost two days, no one had had the presence of mind (and by no one, I mean me, the screaming, cursing, child-birthing bitch from hell) to think ahead to what I would need to know after the baby was born. I didn't know how to feed a baby, burp a baby, change a baby, or wash a baby. I didn't know you had to support a baby's neck in the beginning and be careful of the soft spot on the top of their head. I didn't know that they were supposed to sleep on their side, or maybe their back, but definitely not their stomach, and when they got stuffed up, you had to use this thing that looked like a rubber egg with a nozzle on the end to suck the snot out of their noses. I had no idea how that gnarly black thing in the middle of his stomach was going to magically turn into a belly button, or how I was going to keep him from peeing straight up into my face every time I changed his diaper. There were a thousand things I didn't know that I didn't even know I needed to know. But right then, all I knew was that my child was hungry, and I had no idea how to feed him. I finally understood the old adage, "How do you get water from a stone?"

Sensing my complete lack of knowledge in this area, the nurse sat me up, thrust a pillow behind me, and stuck my son on my boob like he was a piece of Velcro and I was the matching looped side. And then, surprisingly, the Velcro latched on and lunch was served.

"Look at that," I exclaimed. "Five minutes old and he already knows what to do better than I do." I turned to my husband who had been silently watching this scenario from the husband chair in the back of the hospital room. "He's a genius," I crowed. "Better start putting money away for Harvard."

"Yeah," he drawled skeptically. "Let's see how long it takes the genius to get potty trained before we pick out a college for him."

• • •

Right after the ceremonial first feeding, the four grandparents assembled in my hospital room.

"I want to introduce you to your grandson, Joshua Drew Beckerman," I announced elatedly.

"You guys do good work," said my father-in-law admiringly as he took the baby from me.

"Look, he's making eye contact already! He's going to be

very smart!" exclaimed my mother-in-law. My mother nodded
in agreement.

"Who's he named for?" asked my dad. It was not an unexpected question. In the Jewish religion we're supposed to
name our children for a close relative that had recently passed
to that great gefilte fish bowl in the sky. Unfortunately, we'd
had a streak of longevity in our family and the only close relative that had died recently was my grandfather, Jack. Since
then, a half-dozen babies had been born in our family and as
a result of this tradition, we now had Jill, Jon, Justin, Jordan,
and Jay. Obviously Josh was named for Jack and in my
postpartum-induced manic/depressive state, I was irked that I
had to point that out.

"He's named for George Foreman," I said dryly. "The
greatest boxer who ever lived."

"But that's a 'G' name," observed my dad.

"G, J . . . whatever."

"He's not a family member," pointed out my mother.

"True, but he did invent a terrific grill which we use *all* the
time."

"Is George Foreman even Jewish?" my mother asked
my dad.

"Maybe he converted like Sammy Davis Jr. did," replied
my father-in-law.

I sighed and turned to Nurse Bob Marley and told her I
had to pee.

While the family passed the baby around like a plate of
hors d'oeuvres, I hauled my no-longer-pregnant-but-still-
ginormous body over to the bathroom and plunked down on
the toilet. I waited. Nothing happened.

"Nothing is happening," I yelled to Nurse Bob Marley.

She came into the bathroom and looked at me sitting on the can.

"What's da matter?"

"I really, really have to go but it won't come out."

She made some tsk-tsk noises. "Dat's cuz you had da cat'erer in so long while da little man was trying to come out," she explained.

My husband poked his head in the bathroom. "What's up?"

"I can't pee," I said.

"She had da cat'erer in too long," explained the nurse.

"What's wrong with Tracy?" I heard my dad yell from the hospital room.

"She can't pee," my husband called back to the room.

"What?" I heard someone ask.

"Tracy can't pee!" yelled my husband.

"Hey, honey, I don't think they heard you in New Jersey." I sighed.

"Sorry," he said.

I looked up at the nurse again. "So what do I do?" I wondered. My bladder felt so full I thought my eyeballs were going to turn yellow. I remembered when I was little and I had seen a street littered with bird feathers. My older brother had told me that if birds can't pee, they explode in midair. I thought about how sad it would be if I exploded only hours after giving birth and left my newborn son motherless. I also felt bad about not getting to eat the full box of postpartum chocolate Pop-Tarts I had waiting for me at home.

Nurse Bob Marley thought for a minute and then she turned on the sink faucets full blast.

"Tssss," she said, mimicking the sound of the running water.

"Huh?"

"*Tssss,*" she said again over the water running in the sink. "Tink of Niagara Falls!"

I laughed and then all of a sudden, pee slowly tinkled out of me.

"I'm peeing!" I shouted.

"She's peeing!" announced my husband.

A cheer went up in the hospital room. My son would have his mother. And I would have my Pop-Tarts.

● ● ●

Whenever a new baby is born into a Jewish family, it is naturally met with a great deal of joy. When a baby *boy* is born into a Jewish family, it is met with a great deal of joy but also just a tiny bit of dread.

Why dread? Two words: the bris.

No one looks forward to the bris. Being Jews, of course, we are very excited about the abundant platters of salmon, blintzes, and rugelach. But does anyone really look forward to the ritual circumcision of their brand-spanking-new baby? I think not. Especially the mom who, eight days after the birth of her baby, is exhausted, sore, hormonal, leaking milk like a perforated cow, and unable to speak in coherent sentences much less plan a party for all her friends and family, in her house, to watch the slicing of her new son's penis.

According to Jewish law, the father of the baby boy is the one who is supposed to do the deed. However, in a moment of compassion and the realization that the dad would probably pass out cold in the middle of the procedure, God had the good sense to allow for the dad to appoint a stand-in to actually do the circumcision in his stead. The person who is typically appointed is a professional penis snipper called a mohel (pronounced "moyal") and can either be a doctor with some rabbinical training or a rabbi with some medical training. Personally, since it was my son's pee-pee that was going to get cut, I wanted a doctor to do it. If the guy was going to make a mistake, I preferred he screw up on the Hebrew rather than the surgery.

Fortunately, I happened to know a great mohel. He was my brother. Since he was a doctor with some rabbinical training, he was our go-to mohel when my son was born. My brother had actually nipped and tucked every penis born into our family since he'd become a mohel. I'm sure those boys who were all teenagers now would no doubt be horrified to realize that my brother had shaped them all into the young men that they were today.

Anyway, as it usually goes with births, there were a whole bunch of them in the beginning, and then things cooled down once everyone had been married for a while and stopped having sex. In the interim, my brother moved to the West Coast, set up a nice little family practice in Malibu, and did a side business of circumcisions in his spare time on celebrity babies named Zurg.

Moments after my son was born, news spread far and wide that a new baby boy in our family was going to get sliced into the tribe. The good news was my brother, the mohel, was available. The bad news was he was going to have to catch an overnight flight to make the bris.

"If it were *my* son's bris, I don't think I'd want the mohel taking the red-eye," warned my mother. She had arrived when my first contractions had kicked in and stepped in briefly about thirty hours into my labor when I threatened to eviscerate my husband with a spatula if he told me to breathe through the pain one more time.

"Why not?" I asked groggily while I changed my son's diaper and examined his belly-button stub for signs that it was going to fall off.

"Nobody sleeps on the red-eye," she responded.

It took me a minute to fully understand her meaning.

"Oh crap. I didn't think of that."

She shrugged. "Just thought I should point it out."

"Thanks for that, Mom," I responded. "Any other positive thoughts you want to share with me while I recover from the world's largest episiotomy, try to nurse with inverted nipples, and envision my brother falling asleep like a narcoleptic ax murderer just as he lowers the blade onto my son's penis?"

"That's all I got," she said. "Do you think we should get a whole whitefish or whitefish salad?"

After all the guests arrived and we had prepped the baby, my brother took up his post and began the ceremony. My father, the patriarch of the family, was given the honor of holding the baby in his lap while the circumcision was done. Everyone got quiet while the blessings were said, and then the women averted their eyes and I held my breath while my brother made the cut.

"Done!" he announced less than a minute later.

My dad glanced down at the baby in his lap, turned to my brother and proclaimed, "You missed a piece."

"*What?!*" exclaimed my brother.

"You missed a piece," my dad repeated.

"What did he say?" I asked from the back of the room where I stood blubbering from postpartum emotions and the sound of my child crying in pain.

"He said he missed the penis," shouted my grandmother.

"He missed the penis?" I howled. *"How could he miss the penis?"*

"What happened?" asked my aunt Cleo, my grandmother's sister. The two of them were both deaf as a rock and the last people in the world I should have asked for clarification about the state of my son's penis.

"David missed the penis," repeated my grandmother to my great aunt.

"Oy vey!" responded my aunt Cleo. "That's a *Kinahora*."

"A what?" I asked.

"A *Kinahora*. Bad luck. If the mohel misses the penis, it means it will dry up and fall off!"

"No, that's not what it means," argued my grandmother. "It means he will marry a shiksa. A non-Jewish girl! They're used to uncircumcised penises."

"Who married a shiksa?" asked my grandmother's other sister, Aunt Bea, overhearing the tail end of the conversation.

"Nobody," said my grandmother. Then she nodded toward the baby. *"Yet!"*

"Joel!!" I wailed for my husband.

While I frantically tried to find my husband in the throngs of Jews assembled in my tiny apartment, my brother, my mother, my in-laws, a minyan of uncles, a couple of old bubbes, a smattering of younger cousins, and a drunk who came in off the street for some rugelach and whitefish salad all crowded around the baby to look at his penis.

"Gammy said you missed the penis!" I blurted out to my brother after I pushed my way to the front of the crowd.

"No. Not the whole penis. Just a piece. See?" announced my dad, pointing to the penis in question.

"*What??*" I bellowed again.

My brother glared at my dad. "I didn't miss anything!" He bent down to check out his surgical skills.

"It's. A. Piece. Of. *Lint*," he finally affirmed, flicking said lint off the baby's penis.

"Oh," said my dad. "Never mind. Nice work."

I gulped for air as my dad handed the baby back to me. With the drama over, the rest of the family dispersed and descended on the food like they had been wandering in the desert for forty years.

"How are you doing?" asked my brother, when he found me hiccupping in the corner with my freshly circumcised son.

"Oh, you know. Pretty good . . . considering."

"Sorry about all the drama," he said.

"We're Jewish. We invented drama."

"True. But I know it is especially hard on the mom," he replied, giving me a squeeze.

"Only when the mom is surrounded by three deaf aunts who think her son's penis is going to dry up and fall off because her father, who never went to medical school, decided her brother, the mohel, botched the circumcision."

"Yeah, that's not your typical bris," he agreed.

"Hey, but the whitefish salad was good, huh?"

"Delicious."

•　•　•

The true miracle of the bris was not that our son escaped mostly unscathed and that I didn't use the scalpel on any of my family members in the process, but that we had been able to fit thirty-some-odd people in our apartment in the first place. Our apartment only had one bedroom, and a very, very small one at that. When I had first gotten pregnant, we knew we would be unable to afford something with more space and ultimately would need to come up with some creative solution for a nursery or the baby was going to be sleeping in the bathtub. Some of my friends suggested we try co-sleeping with the baby in the bed with us. While I'm sure it works wonderfully for some people, I quickly nixed that idea. Most of the time I don't even like sharing a bed with my husband, much less sharing it with him and a baby. Of course, my husband liked to complain that while I was pregnant, I was the one who was a nightmare to sleep with. Apparently I snored like a foghorn, farted frequently in my sleep, and every time I rolled over, it was like the sinking of the *Titanic*. I would heave my body over with such force, the ensuing mattress wave would bounce my husband right out of bed. We finally agreed that he would not speak of this since I was the one who had to put up with all the vomiting, heartburn, body aches, massive boobs, swollen cankles, and astronomical weight gain for nine months, and all he had to do was make sure there were enough Pop-Tarts in the pantry to feed the cravings of his maniacally hungry pregnant wife. Besides, he knew if he complained about sleeping with me, I would intentionally roll over and smother him.

Since we did, in fact, have a dining room, the obvious choice was to turn it into a nursery. With the exception of the bris, there was little chance we would be hosting massive dinner parties while adjusting to life with a newborn, so we decided to sacrifice the dining room for the greater good of having a place for the baby and all his stuff. Little did we know then that "his stuff" would eventually need a room the size of an airplane hangar to contain it all.

The dining room was actually little more than an alcove

between the kitchen and the living room. In Realtor terms, this is called a "Junior Four" and is supposed to give you more living space than a regular old one bedroom, but in reality is usually no bigger than a utility closet and is just an excuse for them to charge you a lot more money. Still, it was larger than the bathtub, so right before the baby was born we hired a guy to come put up a wall. We filled the space with a crib, a changing table, a rocking chair, a year's worth of diapers, and called it the baby's room.

We found this whole apartment overhaul incredibly amusing when we actually brought the baby home from the hospital and he refused to sleep anywhere except in his car seat, in a stroller, facing the living room window. The living room window thing was actually a medical necessity since he came into the world a luminescent shade of yellow, which meant he needed to get some more vitamin A from the sun to jump-start his liver's bilirubin production. Of course, being the most clueless mother in the world, I had no idea what bilirubin was and when the pediatrician told us the baby needed it, I thought he was referring us to a color specialist named Billy Rubin who would help us adjust the baby's hue from yellow to pink. The fact that my son liked to sleep in a car seat, however, was just his personal preference. After a couple of weeks of this, the pediatrician told us we really needed to get the kid to sleep in the crib so his body could stretch out. Unfortunately the baby did not agree with this plan and he would scream his head off every time we took him out of the car seat and put him in the crib. Eventually I decided the hell with it, and we just put the car seat in the crib, with him in it. Problem solved.

Unfortunately I would soon learn that the issue of where

my son would sleep was going to be the least of our problems. Babies have a really annoying habit of changing the rules on you, and since they can't talk, it's up to you to figure out what the new rules are. Worse yet, sometimes, you find out that the new rule is . . . there are no rules. And then you're screwed.

Chapter 3

If I'm Asleep, I Must Be Dreaming

There are lots of misconceptions about those first few months after the baby is born. In addition to thinking all the pregnancy weight will miraculously disappear once you have the baby, another mistaken belief many new moms have is something called the Perfect Baby Fantasy. A lot of women are under the delusion that their baby, unlike every other baby in the world and the history of mankind, will be different and immediately sleep through the night. When this doesn't happen by the fifth day and you're so tired you feel like your eyeballs are going to fall out, your episiotomy still hurts so you can't go to the bathroom without shrieking, and your feet are still so swollen from the epidural that you can't wear anything but lunch bags for shoes (and if you are one of those women who frowns upon using drugs to ease the pain of childbirth, go read another book), you decide there is no way in hell you will survive this stage of parenthood, much less worry about whether you look cool or not. At this point, it becomes every man for himself, and the person who can fake sleep through the crying at night most convincingly wins. My husband, naturally, was the winner.

Our son actually did sleep through the night the first three nights he was home, which coincidentally were the first three nights we had a baby nurse living with us. Pammy was a boisterous Jamaican nanny our parents had gifted to us when it became clear that my husband and I didn't have a clue what we were doing. Pammy taught us how to change the baby, burp the baby, and duck for cover when he peed up into the air. She had a pretty easy job: For the first three days Josh didn't do much except eat, sleep, and poop. We were pretty cocky and thought we had won the Perfect Baby lottery. But then Pammy left and must have taken the magic fairy dust with her because the day she walked out the door, the baby went ballistic.

I suddenly realized that I did have the perfect baby . . . during the day. But at night he turned into the devil's spawn. He had this night/day thing completely backward and would spend the whole day sleeping and the whole night up crying. Eventually, I ended up the same way, minus the sleeping during the day part, because I needed that time to food shop, clean up, and do so much laundry it seemed I had given birth to an army of exploding infants.

"Doesn't he know he is supposed to sleep at night, when it's dark?" I complained to my husband. "How hard is that to figure out? It was dark in the womb . . . he slept in there for nine months!"

"Those are your rules, not his," he responded wearily. "Don't you remember what my barber Yuri used to say?"

"Yeah, he said, 'Happy wife, happy life.' I'm not very happy, by the way."

"No. The other thing."

"What?" I wondered. I was too sleep deprived to recall anything other than which side the baby had nursed from at the last feeding, and I only knew that because my boobs were uneven.

"He said, 'Baby makes the rules.'"

"That's great," I sighed. "Why don't you call Yuri and tell him the baby has decided he wants a Russian barber to come over here and babysit so his parents can get some sleep."

Josh had colic, and the only thing that soothed him was to be in motion. If he wasn't moving, he wasn't happy. From about eleven p.m. at night until four a.m. every morning he would cry and I would try to find a way to keep him moving. First I would push him back and forth in his stroller. When the stroller stopped working, I'd move him to the windup bouncy seat. After half an hour of that, I would relocate him to the electric swing. Next I would put him in his car seat on top of a running washing machine. Then we would start the whole thing over again. After two weeks of this, I finally carried my crying child into my bedroom and at the top of my lungs I screamed at my sleeping husband, *If you don't get up and help me, I am throwing him out the window!* We lived on the first floor of our apartment building, so it wasn't much of a threat, but from that moment on, my husband and I shared the work at night.

• • •

Having a baby that cries nonstop for a month straight can make you understand why so many people end up as only children.

With my nerves completely frayed from so little sleep and all the crying (mine and the baby's) it was hard enough to maintain my emotional stability much less think about trying to regain some of my pre-baby coolness. Putting on my old clothes was not even a consideration, of course, because (a) nothing fit, (b) the stuff that might possibly have fit was buried under a mountain of baby gear, and (c) within thirty seconds of putting on anything that did fit and was remotely cool, it would be covered in spit-up, pee, poop, or a stunning combination of all three. Not that I had anyone or anything to get dressed up for, anyway. I wasn't going out and my son certainly didn't care if I was wearing the latest Missoni frock or a pair of old Penn State sweats. The baby was an equal-opportunity spitter-upper and would just as soon spew on my designer clothes as my ducky bathrobe. Had I been less tired and more entrepreneurial, I might have thought to invent an overpriced, extra-large bib with a fancy nametag on it and marketed it to new city parents to wear to protect their expensive clothes from their upchucking babies.

The "not going out" thing was actually a new concept to us. Prior to having a baby, my husband and I had been the quintessential city couple: we ate out every night, went to lots of cool art galleries and show openings, and had nothing in the fridge except beer, leftover Chinese food, and yogurt that had expired around the time Bush was in office (the first Bush, that is). Because we lived close to so many movie theaters, our favorite thing to do was go out on a Saturday afternoon, do a double feature, and gorge ourselves on popcorn and Twizzlers. Not surprisingly, we had actually been at the movies the day I went into labor with my son. While it may not be the most opportune place to have your water break, a movie is a great place to have contractions, especially if it is an action flick with lots of explosions and you can time your contractions to happen every time something loud blows up on screen. Unfortunately, it became clear that if we stayed for the end of the movie, my son would have been born at a Loews Cineplex 5 instead of the hospital as planned, so we left after the first half and never saw the end.

Seeing the rest of the movie was certainly not on the top of our list of things to do after the baby was born, but when he turned one month old and my in-laws offered to watch him for a few hours one night, my husband and I decided to take them up on it and go out to finish the movie. I actually didn't really care what the heck we did . . . I was just so excited to get out of the house, without the baby, and let someone else try to get him to stop crying for a few hours. Of course I felt incredibly guilty for feeling this way and knew that the only reason I felt incredibly guilty was because I was so tired and wrung out from being so tired and wrung out all this time. In therapy terms, I think this is what they call a classic New Parent Conundrum. Fortunately it usually resolves itself by the time your child starts sleeping through the night or you abandon your family and go live on an island in the South Pacific, whichever comes first.

While the issue of who was going to watch the baby was solved, the issue of what I was going to wear for our date night was still hanging out there like my flabby post-baby belly hung over the waistband of my pants.

"How about these? These are cute!" proclaimed my husband, holding up a pair of black jeans that he found on the top of a reject pile on our bed.

"Are you serious?" I demanded. "I can't wear those. Those are maternity jeans!"

"Isn't this the pile of clothes that fit you?" he asked innocently. He had no idea what dangerous waters he had tread into. He would have been safer covered in chum and swimming with great white sharks.

"Yes, they fit," I said icily. "But that's the problem. I *don't* fit into my old clothes. I *do* fit into my maternity clothes. But I do *not* want to wear clothes that I wore when I was pregnant."

"Why not?"

"'Cuz I'm not pregnant anymore!" I bellowed.

He dropped the pants and slowly backed out of the room as though he had just stumbled upon an armed bank robbery or some other extremely dangerous situation in progress.

"Just let me know when you're ready, honey," he said softly. "I'm gonna go wait someplace safe. Like Brooklyn."

I glared at the clothes on my bed. I hated the maternity clothes for still fitting. I hated my old clothes for not fitting. And I hated all those pregnant women who had their babies and were back in their old clothes in two weeks. I wasn't sure who those women were, but they were making the rest of us look bad and for that I decided they should be strung up by their skinny jeans and shot.

•　•　•

Going into a warm, dark room with plush comfortable chairs when you haven't slept for a month may not be the best plan for actually seeing a movie, but it is a great plan for catching up on your sleep. We bought tickets for the same movie we had started to see when I went into labor, got through the

same first half we saw before my water broke, and then
promptly fell asleep and missed the same second half we didn't
see the first time around. Although we were disappointed that
we still didn't know how the movie ended, we felt more
refreshed than we had in weeks. Giddy with rest, we practically
skipped back to our apartment after the film to relieve my
in-laws from babysitting duty.

As we stood outside the apartment door, I stopped for a
minute and listened.

"Do you hear that?" I asked my husband.

"What? No. I don't hear anything," he said.

"I know. That's the point. No crying. The baby's not crying," I said incredulously. "I think your parents killed him!!"

I threw open the apartment door and ran in. My in-laws
were relaxing on the couch, watching TV.

"Where's Josh?" I demanded.

"He's sleeping," responded my mother-in-law. "He's a good
sleeper!" she said.

"No. No, he's not! He's a terrible sleeper," I argued. "He
must be dead." I looked around for the car seat stroller and saw
it parked in the corner of the living room. A sense of gloom
washed over me as I approached the stroller. I drew near it and
then peered in. There, in the car seat, was my son, sleeping
soundly . . . with a pacifier in his mouth.

"Aaaccckkkk! You gave him . . . a *pacifier*!" I yelled.

My in-laws looked stricken. They exchanged frightened
glances. "He was crying and we knew he wasn't hungry and
we saw a bunch of them on the changing table so we thought
he could have one," my mother-in-law explained. My
father-in-law vigorously nodded his head up and down.

"They were in the hospital goody bag, but we decided not to use them!" I explained. "We heard stories . . . about babies . . . and pacifiers. Horrible stories of three-year-olds who still needed them." I lowered my voice. "They get *addicted*."

My mother-in-law smiled with relief. "It's okay. Babies need to suck. When he finds his finger, he won't need the pacifier," she assured me.

"But what if he never finds his finger? Or he prefers that stupid rubber plug and he won't give it up. He could go to *college* with it," I wailed.

I imagined my son struggling with a life of pacifier addiction. It would start as one Binky, but soon he would progress to multiple Binkies. He'd start needing them to get through exams, job interviews, and presentations. He'd have a pacifier in his mouth on his wedding day. He'd fight his new baby for it. He would be forced to admit that his life had become unmanageable and he'd become powerless over the pacifier. Finally, one day, there he'd be, having to remove it to take the oath of office as president. It was clearly a pacifier nightmare waiting to happen.

At this point, my husband awoke from whatever stupor he was in that had been induced by the sight of our baby sucking hard on a Hello Kitty Binky.

"I guess it couldn't hurt for him to use it for a little while, you know, just to help him get through this colicky thing," he backpedaled. I gave him a death stare. We had agreed: no Binky, but in an instant, my husband sold his soul to the pacifier devil for some peace and quiet and uninterrupted sleep. I had to admit; it did seem to soothe the baby and looked like it might be a much better solution that staying up all night and moving the baby from the bouncy seat to the washing machine. But somehow, I suspected, the Binky solution was eventually going to bite me in my large, postpartum ass.

· · ·

Two months after the baby was born, I was no longer pukey, but I was fat, tired, and cranky. (I'm pretty sure these were three of the original seven dwarfs who were later edited out by Disney.) As I had predicted, the pacifier solution turned into the negative sleep association from hell. The baby got so used to sucking himself to sleep that he couldn't fall asleep without the rubber plug. The biggest problem, however, wasn't falling asleep. The biggest problem was staying asleep. Whenever Josh would wake up in the middle of the night, if there was no Hello Kitty Binky in his mouth, he'd start to cry. Since this usually happened between three-hour feedings, it meant he would sleep for an hour and then wake up crying for his pacifier and then wake up an hour later crying for a meal. In case you lost count, this meant I had to get up and go to him almost every hour to either feed him, change him, or stick the pacifier back in his mouth. Although duct tape was, at one point, discussed as an option, we instead decided that in the long run and in the interest of his future presidential career, Josh needed to give up the Binky.

It had been a brief love affair but an intense one, and he was not going to give up his adored pacifier without a fight. At first we tried the cold-turkey method, but after two solid hours of crying, we finally gave in. The next day I called the pediatrician.

"The baby won't sleep without a pacifier," I told him.

"Yeah? How's that working for you?" he wondered. He was one of those newfangled breeds of New York City doctors who wore Birkenstocks to the office, had a bunch of stuffed wild things clipped to his stethoscope, and went by the name Dr. Steve. Our conversations tended to be less doctor and patient and more cool medical guy and new idiot mom.

"Not so good," I admitted. "Whenever he falls asleep, the pacifier pops out of his mouth and then he wakes up and cries for it again."

"Uh-huh," he replied knowingly.

". . . So, I was wondering if you could recommend a book to read on the topic or maybe prescribe a methadone-type pacifier replacement system."

He gave me the book.

This particular sleep theory recommended that you take the pacifier away, but go into the baby's room at timed intervals and reassure him with a pat on the back and a soothing voice that he was fine, that Mommy and Daddy were here, and that, yes (!), he could fall asleep without the damn plug in his mouth. Okay, that last part wasn't part of the program, but that was the intent.

The problem with this method is it is only successful if you actually follow it. Of course this makes sense, but imagine you are a new mom with wild hormones, leaky breasts, and perpetual exhaustion, and you have to listen to your baby wail inconsolably for something that you know will soothe him, but you can't give it to him because some stupid sleep doctor told you the baby needs to figure out how to fall asleep on his own without any external source to help him do it.

Yeah, I didn't handle it too well, either.

This is why my husband had to barricade me in the bedroom while we taught the baby how to sleep without the Binky.

For all of the drama, it only took two nights. And then from that moment on, Josh slept soundly, without a Binky, a blankie, or a finger, through the night.

Or at least for two hours until he woke up to be fed.

Chapter 4

Hi-Ho, Hi-Ho, It's Off to Work with My Breast Pump I Go . . .

By the time Josh was three months old, we had settled into a pretty good rhythm at home, but I still felt unsettled. Although I loved being with him, I was pretty sure the only way I was going to get my groove back was if I returned to work. This was not a surprise to me or my husband. It had always been my intention to go back to work after my maternity leave. Having worked for ten years and having killed off numerous people to get to the top of my career as a high-powered TV executive, I had thought that nothing, especially not motherhood, would keep me from reclaiming my rightful spot on the career throne.

Finding a nanny was the easy part. Although she had only been with us for three days, we had loved our former baby nurse, Pammy, so much that we had her come back and babysit on occasion while I was still on maternity leave and my husband and I thought somewhat delusionally that we could go to dinner without falling asleep face-first in our food. Dinner out with three hours of sleep might not have been the smartest decision, but keeping Pammy in the fold was a no-brainer. When the time came to hire a full-time nanny, Pammy was the obvious choice.

I was thrilled to pick my old life back up where I had left it three months earlier. My coworkers were happy to have the old, productive me back, in place of the vomiting, bovine-sized pod that had taken over my body for nine months, and I was happy to be back someplace where I actually knew what I was doing. What I had not counted on, however, was feeling so bone-achingly tired when I got back, so disinterested in my job, and so utterly envious of the time my nanny was spending with my son.

While I sat at my computer writing news promo scripts, I thought of my son. While I sat in the edit bay producing promos, I thought of my son. And I thought of my son when I sat in production meetings pretending to listen to asinine news producers talk about the latest story for the evening news about how the local dry cleaners could be poisoning you. For someone who had only been around a little more than three months, Josh had somehow managed to take up a lot of real estate in my heart in a very short time. It had taken me longer than that to fall in love with my husband, and he'd never spit up on me or peed on my boss the first time they met.

I sucked it up, threw myself into my job, and somehow managed to get through the first two months back at work. But by the time Josh was five months old, that little gnawing feeling that I was blowing it by not being home with my son became a full-on Abominable Snowman–sized realization.

Still, I was determined to make work, work because (a) we needed the money, (b) it was an incredibly cool job, and (c) I just didn't think I was stay-at-home-mom material as evidenced by my complete lack of maternal knowledge and inability to sing one damn *Barney* song.

To diminish my working-mom guilt, I had decided to continue breastfeeding and bought a pump to use at work. Fortunately, I had an actual office, instead of just a cubicle, so I was saved the embarrassment of having to milk the cow in the restroom. Unfortunately, my office had paper-thin walls and was surrounded by every edit bay and cubicle in the newsroom. Even amidst the sounds of promo writers typing and news editors editing police sirens into segments, there was no mistaking the rhythmic whoosh-whooshing of my breast pump emptying my size H udders into the bottles. Even if I wanted to blend back in seamlessly with my pre-baby work self, there was no way to do it when it sounded like a dairy farm in my office. As if that wasn't bad enough, I was often so busy running interference from the newsroom to the promo department that I would be late emptying *the girls* and they would start to leak though my tragically uncool nursing blouses. Of course I knew I was not the first woman to go back to work right after having a baby while I was still nursing. But I was the first woman in *my* office to do so, and the mostly male staff was at a loss for how to handle a ragingly hormonal, postpartum coworker who would routinely appear at staff meetings with two wets spots on the front of her shirt. Cool as this might be in some parts of the world where breast milk stains are a fashion statement, it had not quite caught on yet in New York City offices, and I was pretty sure that the other people in my department were not staring at my lactating mammaries because they were in awe of my nouveau style statement. For a while I tried to ignore the looks and remember that I was doing something good for my son. But one day as I was reviewing the script of a junior producer, I looked up to see him staring intently at my breasts and I snapped.

"Unless you need some milk for your coffee, I suggest you focus on this sorry-ass script you wrote rather than being fixated on my leaking boobs."

He turned a nifty shade of red and slunk out of my office. A moment later my boss's head popped in.

"Hey, Jax," I greeted him brightly.

"Got a sec?" he wondered.

I stuffed a couple of tissues down my bra to soak up the flow of milk and followed him into his office.

"So, how's it going?" he asked nonchalantly as he eased into the chair behind his desk.

"How's it going at work or how's it going in general?" I responded innocently, plopping down into a chair across from him.

"Both."

"Good," I lied. "You know, still trying to find a way to balance it all. Work, new baby, leaky boobs."

He smiled knowingly. We had a pretty comfortable relationship born out of the mutual respect we had for each other both personally and professionally. He had helped me grow creatively when I was a newbie in the business and groomed me for the number-two position I now held, knowing full well I was gunning for his job. I was also enormously in awe of how, in the midst of all the chaos in the newsroom, he always managed to be pretty Zen. But mostly what I liked about him was his integrity. He defied the backstabbing and alliances so common in the TV business and did what he thought was right, including promoting me when I was pregnant because I deserved it, but also so I would have a job that had more regular hours, enabling me to spend more time with my new son.

"Tougher than you thought it would be, huh?" he remarked kindly.

I nodded. "I thought I could just pop out the baby, hand him off to a nanny, and come back to work. I had no idea I would feel so conflicted about being here," I admitted. I absentmindedly played with a magnetic sculpture toy he had on his desk, suddenly realizing with horror that I had molded the magnets into a pair of breasts. I quickly smushed it and sat back in my chair.

"I remember my former wife went through the same thing thirty-something years ago," my boss recalled, oblivious to the magnetic boobs I had created. "She loved her job, but she hated being away from the kids."

"How'd she handle it?"

"She quit her job."

I raised an eyebrow. "Is that what you think I should do?" I asked, squirming nervously in my chair. Did I really want to know the answer to that question?

"No. It would be a real loss here for us if you left. A real loss for me," he clarified. "But I get that you have *two* jobs now. One here and one at home."

"I just don't feel like I'm doing either job very well right now," I admitted.

"I think you're handling it all great," he said. "If you're half the mom you are the promo producer, I'm sure Josh is thriving."

I wanted to hug this man. Or kill him, hide the body, and steal his job. Either one would be good.

"If there's anything you want to change to make it work better, let me know," he said sympathetically.

I smiled. "Thanks!"

He thought for a minute. "You know, you live pretty close to the station. Would it help or hurt for you to go home occasionally for lunch? Check in? Reconnect?"

"I don't know," I mused. "I guess I could try it and see how it goes." I looked down at my milk-stained blouse. "At the very least, it would give me a chance to change my shirt."

•   •   •

As I thought about it, I decided that going home for lunch was a great idea. I could touch base with my son and give him a hug. Plus, I had read all the requisite new-mommy handbooks and learned that if you have a nanny, it is important to make the occasional surprise visit home to be sure everything is going well. Of course I trusted Pammy completely so I was really not concerned that I would find anything worrisome going on. However, as I walked the ten blocks home from the TV station to our apartment, I became more and more convinced that things were not as wonderful as they seemed. By the time I got to our building I was sure the baby was being neglected and mistreated and was on a boat to a foreign country to be sold into infant slavery. I hurled myself at the apartment door and then stopped to chastise myself for being so paranoid. But as I put the key in the lock, I suddenly heard screaming inside. Horrified, I flung the door open, ran into the living room, and yelled, *"Stop!"* Five pairs of nanny eyes turned and looked at me from the couch where four nannies and Pammy were sitting watching some game show on TV and eating Chinese food while my son and four other babies happily played on the floor. All the nannies stared at me with chopsticks and lo mein frozen in midair while the game show contestant who had just won a brand-new living room set continued to scream for joy on TV.

"Everything okay?" asked Pammy.

"Um, yeah," I said blushing furiously. "I, um, forgot my breast pump." I scooped up the baby, smothered him with kisses, and then ran into the bedroom and slammed the door. Then I made loud whooshing noises with my cheeks to sound like the breast pump, which I had actually left at work. I picked up the phone and called my husband.

"Hi (whoosh, whoosh). It's me (whoosh, whoosh)."

"What the heck are you doing?" he asked.

"I'm home (whoosh, whoosh)," I said. "I came to check up on the nanny (whoosh, whoosh)."

"No, I mean, what is that sound?" he asked.

"What sound (whoosh, whoosh)?"

"That whooshing sound," he demanded.

"Oh (whoosh, whoosh). I want her to think I am using my breast pump (whoosh, whoosh)."

"What? Why? Oh, never mind," he said in resignation. He knew I was a tired, cranky, hormonal mess and it was probably safer not to know why I did the things I did.

I took a deep breath and then I blurted out what I had been feeling for weeks. "I'm very unhappy (whoosh, whoosh)."

"Could you please stop that whooshing sound!" he yelled.

"Sorry."

He took a breath. "Why are you unhappy, honey?" he asked me softly.

"I thought I wanted to go back to work, but I hate my job and I miss our son and *the nanny is having a better time than*

I am," I cried. Then I went back to whooshing to cover up my cries.

There was silence on the other end of the phone for what seemed like a really long time.

"Hello?" I asked, thinking he'd hung up and run out to find a young bimbo who wasn't tired and cranky to replace me with.

"I'm very unhappy, too," he admitted.

"You are?" I wondered with astonishment.

"Yes."

"I want to quit my job." I gulped.

"Okay. Let's talk tonight."

Chapter 5

All I Need Is a Really Large Bra and a Bigger Apartment to Keep It In

Quitting my job entirely was not really an option since we needed at least part of my income to stay in the city. Fortunately my boss agreed to let me freelance for the station part-time and write scripts from home. It was something I could do in the late morning and afternoon while Josh napped, and in the early evening after he went to bed. It worked out well from the time that he was six months until he was ten months old and it seemed like a win-win situation: I got to spend time with my son, I was still able to earn some money, and no one from work would see me in uncool clothes covered in breast milk and baby food. But as he got bigger, the strains of having a baby in the city started to reveal themselves. And by strains, I specifically mean our apartment. The mountain of baby stuff that had begun to accumulate was overwhelming and it wasn't long before it became obvious that we needed to make a change.

"We need more room," stated my husband after he tripped over my son's massive stationary activity center. In case you are not familiar with this interesting contraption, it looks a little like a small, plastic UFO, but it is neither a personal spaceship nor a weird kind of baby gym apparatus that is sold on QVC at two in the morning. It is one of those things you put your non-standing kid in so he can stand but not actually go anywhere. It bounces and it rocks and it's really fun for the kid, but it hurts a lot when you smash your toe into it in the middle of the night on your way to the bathroom.

We had one of these activity centers and a bouncy seat and a swing and a doorway jumper. We had so many bouncy-jumpy things, I was convinced my son would grow up to be in Cirque du Soleil. Then there was the high chair, the portable playpen/crib, and three strollers: a jogging stroller, a car seat stroller, and a regular stroller, because no city baby should have less than three sets of wheels . . . especially when his parents don't even own a car. We had a plastic kitchen, and a plastic tool bench, and plastic playhouse so that the minute he could walk, our son would be able to pretend he was Wolfgang Puck or Bob Vila or Pee-wee Herman. Then there were the various rocking horses, rocking chairs, and a giant teepee, the must-have accessory for every fashionable city baby–cum–Native American. All this stuff was mixed in with all our stuff, and us, in a 650-square-foot apartment. We were literally bursting at the seams.

I had also begun to realize that getting around the city with a toddler, without a car, was a monstrous undertaking. Every time we went out, I hauled so much stuff with me I felt like a

Bedouin. If we'd been real Bedouins, at least we would have had a camel to help lug the stuff around. Unfortunately this was not a possibility for us since we lived in a pet-free apartment building. Not that there was room in our apartment for a camel, anyway, even if it only had one hump. I'm pretty sure even a small llama couldn't have fit in our apartment, nor handled the load of stuff I needed to take with me for a short outing. There was the massive diaper bag with enough wipes, dipes, and clothing changes to take care of two dozen exploding babies; the infant carrier to wear across my chest because it wasn't enough of a strain on my back to haul around size H-cup breasts, I needed to add a fifteen-pound baby to the load; the collapsible stroller with the car seat insert so I could switch from subway or bus to taxi when I got tired of standing because no one would give up their seat for a woman with a baby and a mountain of gear; and of course, the infant himself. When you add into that whatever groceries, dry cleaning, or shopping you pick up during your outing, you realize you have to be a mom the size of a sumo wrestler to manage all the stuff. Of course, with all the extra weight I was still carrying from being pregnant, it was clear that I might qualify for sumo status anyway.

Still, I was reluctant to give up the perks of city life. We were never at a loss for what to do, everything we needed was within a three-block radius of our apartment, and if we really didn't want to go out or we didn't feel well, we could get a pizza or Valium delivered to our home at three o'clock in the morning.

The deciding factor finally came when Josh was ten months old. The newsroom downsized, half the staff got fired, and the freelancers were given the choice to either work full-time, sans benefits, or leave.

I took what was behind door number two. This left us with one income and not a lot of housing choices.

"I think we should consider moving to the suburbs," said my husband one night as he tried to squeeze past me and the baby in the kitchen to get a beer from the fridge.

"Noooo. Not the su-burbbbsss," I said with mock horror. I was feeding Josh and we were both covered in food. He had just entered that stage where he was more interested in wearing the food than eating it. I had given up on wearing anything even remotely fashionable for this chore because every time I fed him, eighty percent of the food ended up all over me, my son, the high chair, most of the kitchen, and half of New York.

"I know it's not as cool as the city," said my husband, finding a beer in the fridge. He turned, smacked his head on a cabinet I'd left open, and dropped the beer. We both sighed as it rolled under the high chair and into a puddle of strained peas. "But we could have a house, and a yard for the kids to play in and a nice street for them to ride their bikes, and our neighbors would bring over cookies when we moved in."

"Where are you thinking of moving to . . . Mayberry?" I asked him. I reached down, grabbed the beer, and handed it to him.

"It will be quieter, too," he said. As if to punctuate his point, the sound of a police car and ambulance screeched through our living room, someone's car alarm went off, garbage collectors smashed recyclable bottles into their trucks, and a crazy man bellowed obscenities outside our window. I'm sure he was probably complaining about all the noise.

"Don't kid yourself there, Opie," I retorted. "The suburbs have car alarms, police cars, and garbage collectors, too. Plus, there are lawn mowers and weed whackers and electric tree saws."

". . . But no crazy people yelling obscenities," he said.

"Yeah, till I move in."

I relocated the food-covered child to one of his bouncy-jumpy things so he could bounce and jump and I could hose down the high chair and the kitchen. My husband popped the top off his beer and foam shot out of the bottle and straight onto my shirt.

"Oh jeez, I'm sorry, honey," he cried, grabbing a dish towel to wipe me off.

"Forget it," I said, pulling off the dirty shirt. "I needed something to wash the strained peas off my shirt, anyway."

"We would have more than one bathroom," he continued. "We would have more than one closet . . ."

He knew my buttons. I hated having to wait to use our only bathroom, especially after my husband used it on Mexican fiesta dinner night. And I had to keep most of my clothes in storage in the apartment building's basement and rotate them in because we only had one closet for the three of us that we shared with the vacuum cleaner.

"A bigger kitchen . . ."

I nodded unconsciously.

". . . And of course we would get a car."

A car? A car to carry all our crap in? A car to get me to the supermarket when we were out of milk and it was pouring rain outside? A car to lull my son to sleep in when he wouldn't take a nap and we both needed one? A car would be great. We couldn't afford a car in the city because the parking was almost as much as our rent. But in the suburbs we would have a garage. And bathrooms. And closets. It was beginning to sound pretty good. I could feel myself begin to warm to the idea. All I needed to close the deal was an agreement that we would move someplace close, someplace cool, someplace with charm . . .

"How about we look in New Jersey?" he suggested.

You know, sharing a bathroom isn't so bad, I thought.

.   .   .

As a New York City girl, I was understandably shaken when my husband suggested we move to New Jersey. New Jersey wasn't a state; it was a punch line. To those of us from outside the Garden State, it seemed to be populated by big Italian families with sixteen relatives all named Anthony and Jewish families that kept kosher at home and then went out for bacon cheeseburgers on Friday nights. It was a place where men had more hair on their backs than on their heads and could bench-press twice their IQs in weights. Where women wore skintight animal prints and dressed their little dogs in people clothes. And where half the clients getting manicures at one of the sixteen million nail salons were men with diamond initial pinky rings.

Of course, in reality, there were just as many dumb muscle-heads, trampy-looking women, and stupidly dressed dogs in New York. But it was much more fun to single out New Jersey and make sweeping generalizations about the people there, especially if you were married to one of them.

Needless to say, my concern in moving to New Jersey was not that I wouldn't be able to get a seat at the nail salon, but that I would become one of those people that *other* people made fun of. Even though I knew I would never attempt to

squeeze my post-baby body into a pair of animal-print leg-
gings, develop a Jersey accent, or make Bruce Springsteen my
ringtone, I still harbored the fear that having a New Jersey zip
code would instantly devalue my cool rating among my New
York friends to such an extent that I would be banned from
ever buying a multi-ride subway card again. Although my husband assured me that I would be cool no matter where we
lived, I was pretty sure that the suburbs plus New Jersey plus
motherhood would no doubt destroy whatever vestiges of hipness I had remaining that had not already gone out the door
with my size-eight skinny jeans.

Of course, New Jersey wasn't the only suburb on the table.
My husband had suggested New Jersey because he had grown
up in New Jersey and his parents were still there. We both
knew parental proximity was a definite plus for young couples
with new babies. Most of my city friends who had relocated
to the suburbs had moved close to one set of parents or the
other for the obvious babysitting benefits.

Although my parents had moved down to Florida, like many
former New Yorkers, they soon got a small place up north in
Westchester County not far from where I grew up to wait out
the Floridian heat and the hurricanes during the summer
months. Besides escaping the weather, they thought it would
be nice to come up here and do something different than they
do in Florida. I thought that meant going into the city and seeing shows. But they just meant playing golf and stealing sugar
packets from restaurants in New York, rather than in Florida.

Although Westchester had a cooler reputation than
New Jersey, there were a lot of similarities to the two locales.
The taxes were identical in both areas, the schools were
comparable, and the commute into New York City was about

the same. But as we went back and forth, my husband finally brought it down to its simplest terms:

"If we move to New Jersey, my parents will help us out with the kids," he proclaimed. "If we move to Westchester, you'll have to pick up your dad's dry cleaning."

While I couldn't argue that point with him, I realized that the bigger issue was not whether we moved to the New Jersey suburbs or the New York suburbs, but that we moved to *any* suburbs. Although I agreed with my husband that it would be great for all of us to have more room, to have a street for our son and future children to ride their bikes in, and a yard to throw a Frisbee to our eventual dog, I felt a huge loss at the idea of moving out of the city. The city was the place where I got my first taste of independence. It was where I discovered myself, my career, my passion for the arts and fashion, and of course, the man I would desperately, passionately fall in love with and marry. The city was alive and inspiring and sometimes rough and scary, but always exciting and I was afraid if I moved to the suburbs, I would lose all of those things, and myself, in the process. I knew intellectually that a move to the suburbs was the right one for our family, but emotionally I was scared as hell and reluctant to give up my old life, as uncomfortable as it was becoming. The truth was, I had already started down that path by having a baby and quitting my job and there really was no turning back. I had to invent a new normal and it seemed that life included not just a philosophical change but a geographical one as well.

Although it was clear we needed to make a change, I thought it would be rash to make such a big decision without consulting some experts. So I called my mom.

My parents were professional suburbanites. They both grew up in the burbs, raised three kids in the burbs, and lived there for thirty-five years before deciding to relocate to the Jewish promised land, otherwise known as Florida. Truth be told, they had no choice: My dad turned seventy and started wearing his pants under his armpits, so they had to go. No place else would have him dressed like that.

We were pretty disappointed when they told us they were moving if for no other reason than we had counted on the free babysitting. Naturally they were a little conflicted about moving so far away from their new grandchild, but ultimately it came down to the fact that my dad said he was tired of shoveling snow. Plus, he said that now that he was older and his blood was thinner, he really couldn't tolerate the cold. I told him he was confused. It wasn't his blood that was thinner. It was his hair.

"Joel thinks we should leave the city and get a house in New Jersey," I said to my mom over the phone.

"It's a good idea," she agreed. "I mean the leaving-the-city part. Not necessarily the moving-to-New-Jersey part."

"What's wrong with New Jersey?" I asked innocently.

"Nothing," she sighed. "New Jersey is fine. You know, if you don't mind living next door to Tony Soprano."

I shook my head in disbelief.

"You do know that Tony Soprano is a fictional character, right, Mom?"

"Of course I know that," she replied indignantly. "I meant, a guy *like* Tony Soprano."

"You mean a mob guy."

"Yes. They are all over New Jersey," she said assuredly.

"What does that have to do with me moving to the suburbs?" I wondered.

"Nothing. I'm just saying there are lots of questionable people in New Jersey and it might not be the best place to raise a family. Why don't you look out on Long Island, instead?"

"You mean Long Island where the Gotti family lives?"

Silence.

"I don't think there are any mobsters in Westchester," she finally offered.

"Okay, can we forget about where the mobsters live and focus on whether or not I should move to the suburbs in general," I asked.

"I don't think you should be so quick to dismiss this issue," she said. "You could move to the most beautiful suburb in America, piss off your neighbor, and then find out he's a mobster and wants to whack you."

"Mom," I said thoughtfully. "Did you see this on *Law and Order* last night?"

"Maybe."

"I'm not moving next door to a mobster," I assured her.

"But those stories are ripped from the headlines," she protested.

I sighed. "I gotta go. The baby's crying."

"What's wrong?"

"Nothing. Babies cry," I said.

"Check to make sure he doesn't have a rash on the bottom of his feet. It could be hoof-and-mouth disease."

"Did you see that on TV last night, too?" I wondered.

"Maybe."

"Uh-huh. Call you later."

• • •

I really wasn't worried that I might unwittingly move next door to a mobster if we relocated to New Jersey. But I was pretty nervous that we would move next to someone who was tragically unhip, in a town of tragically unhip people, and all of their unhipness would rub off on me. I had friends who had moved to the suburbs from the city and the quick transformation from cool city chick to unhip suburbanite seemed to be inevitable and complete. Not that I was going into this move at the top of my form, by any means. With my current look of covered-with-baby-food couture, lack-of-sleep raccoon eyes, and no-time-to-get-to-the-salon hairstyle, I was about as cool as a Ford Pinto. Actually, this was a pretty good analogy considering the uncanny resemblance that existed between the back of the Pinto and the size of my post-baby butt. Of course, the big difference between the Pinto and me was that I wouldn't blow up if I were rear-ended. I hoped. Still, I assumed that unlike all my friends before me, I might actually be able to retain some of my city hipness when I relocated to the wilds of suburbia if for no other reason than I could not stand the thought of them all saying "I told you so" from the comfort of their big, hunkin' minivans.

While the lack of space was certainly a big consideration in our decision to move out of the city, it was not *the* consideration. The bigger factor was money. Without my income as an uber-hot TV executive, we didn't really have enough money to afford the place we were already living in, much less one that was larger. Since I had this burning desire to repeat the weight gain/vomit fest/boob explosion that I called pregnancy a second time at some point down the road, we knew we either had to move out of our current apartment or run the risk that the physics of having all that baby gear stuffed into a finite space could create a cosmic black hole that would suck us, my son, and all his jumpy things in and spit us out the other side of the universe where, hopefully, there were cooler suburbs than they had here on Earth. While this seemed like a better option than moving to the burbs, I had yet to see Stephen Hawking postulate such a theory and therefore didn't have much faith that it would happen before I got pregnant again. This being the case, I ultimately decided to bite the bullet and consider New Jersey, if only so I could call my mother after we moved and tell her I had met my new neighbor and her name was Carmela.

"Okay, I'm in," I said to my husband at dinner that night.

"In what?"

"I'm in with the idea of us looking at some houses in New Jersey."

"Really?" he said hopefully. "What changed your mind?"

"I pictured myself wearing mom jeans and driving a mini-van to pick up new hair scrunchies at Walmart and it made me quiver with excitement."

"I could see that."

"Seriously," I said seriously. "What happens if I'm transformed into some kind of sad suburbanite with childbearing hips who wears velour jumpsuits that say 'Juicy' across the butt and you fall out of love with me and abandon us for some hot little urban trollop half my age?"

"It'll never happen."

"How do you know?"

"I'm not attracted to urban trollops."

"I used to be an urban trollop," I reminded him.

"Well, my tastes have changed," he said. "Now I'm into hot suburban moms with childbearing hips."

"Any hot suburban mom?"

"No, just you."

"Good to know."

Chapter 6

The Only Good Thing About the Suburbs Is They Deliver Ice Cream to Your Door

My husband pulled the old bait and switch. It was just like those ads for used cars that promise you a sexy convertible for a ridiculously low price, and then when you get to the showroom, they give you some old clunker.

When we talked about moving to the suburbs, I had fantasies of living in a castle. What we got was a cottage. Actually, it was more of a shed. But at least it was a shed with a garage.

It was not, admittedly, my husband's fault. We thought our single income would go a lot further in the suburbs than in the city. But after narrowing down the playing field to a location that was a reasonable distance from New York City, we discovered that you don't get that much more house *close* to the city than you can get apartment *in* the city. Since we had been renting for all of our adult lives, we didn't have anything to sell and therefore we didn't have any money to buy anything bigger than a bread box. So we decided to rent again and hopefully save enough money to be able to buy a house in a few years. Unfortunately, there were not that many great house rental properties. After searching high and low, we finally found a cute house with a cute backyard on a quiet street in a cute New Jersey town (I know . . . that is an oxymoron). The catch was, it had one bathroom and one closet.

Really.

We decided to take the plunge and prayed that we would have enough money to buy a house with more bathrooms before my son started potty training.

The good news was the house had two actual bedrooms *and* a living room *and* a dining room *and* a kitchen and they were all separate rooms unlike our apartment, which had basically been one room divided by toys. The plastic playhouse had separated the living room from the kitchen and the teepee had separated the kitchen from the dining room/baby's room. When people asked me what style of decorating we had, I said it was Early Modern Playskool.

As small as it was, the house had a lot of charm in a compact, puce-colored-aluminum-siding, shag-carpeting kind of way. Based on the steepness of the staircase, it was clear the house had been a ranch that had been converted to a two-story. I thought the previous owners who decided to do the conversion must have been dwarves if the extraordinarily low ceiling height on the second level was any indication. They also, apparently, had been dwarves with great bladder control because the master bedroom was on the second level and the lone bathroom was on the first. While this was very convenient for my son who lived on the first level and didn't even need the toilet, it was less so for me when I later got pregnant and had to hurl myself down the staircase whenever I had to puke or pee in the middle of the night.

Charming as the new house was and excited as I was for our new suburban adventure, I found myself mourning our life in the city before we even left. As the moving van pulled away from our apartment with us in our new, used Buick LeSabre following behind, I looked back at my soon-to-be former life and cried. When we got to our new house in the suburbs, I put my son down on grass for the first time, and he cried.

We were off to a roaring start.

I had grown up in the suburbs, so it's not like this was a completely foreign experience to me. I was raised in a nice, mostly Jewish town in Westchester, which is a county encompassing other nice, mostly Jewish towns in the suburbs of New York City. It was there that my two brothers and I learned the fine art of shoplifting bubble gum from the local stationery store, how to make an exploding bottle rocket, and how to swipe ice cream from the back of the Good Humor truck when the ice cream man wasn't looking.

We lived where we did because we needed to be a good commutable distance to New York City where my dad worked. He was an advertising executive and the funniest person I knew. His idea of a good joke was to bring a front door to a housewarming party. My mom worked with special-needs kids, which always made my brothers and I look brilliant in comparison, even if we weren't.

When it came to finding our own spouses, my parents had high expectations for us and strongly suggested I try to find someone rich, Jewish, and normal. I fulfilled my part of the deal by first bringing home a guy twice my age, then a fellow who thought he could make things move with his mind, and finally, a cross-dresser. None of them were rich. None of them were Jewish. And clearly, none of them were normal. Little did they know I was just trying to diminish their expectations so that when I finally did bring home the man who would become my husband, he would seem like the catch of the century. I needn't have suffered through the first three though, because the guy I eventually married was really, actually the sweetest man, ever, on the face of the Earth, *and* he was Jewish. This made my parents deliriously happy and made me a shoo-in for the child most likely to inherit everything in their will.

I really loved growing up in the burbs. There were a ton of kids the same age who lived on my street and we would play outside together all summer under the shadows of the old willow trees until it got dark and our parents would summon us home for dinner. Each family had a different call to bring their wayward child home and we each knew each other's call as well as our own. My folks had a big cowbell that hung on the back porch that they would ring when dinner was ready. My friend Nina's mother had this special whistle for her, which was also, coincidentally the same whistle they used to call in their pet beagle. And my neighbor Jody's folks would yell her name like some farmhands would call the pigs to slop. "Jo-Deeee! Jo-Deeee!" Then our game of steal the flag or dodgeball would start to fall apart as one by one we would be dragged away by a sense of obedience instilled by the threat of bodily harm. For an hour, the street would be quiet as dusk fell and the smell of Hamburger Helper wafted through the neighborhood. Then around six thirty p.m. one more bell would ring and all the kids would come pouring out of their homes one last time. It was the Good Humor man. To this day,

I'm flooded with sweet memories of childhood and petty thievery whenever I hear that bell ring. Of course, I'm sure the price has gone up since then, and it probably doesn't taste as good as I remember. But for me, the Good Humor man is synonymous with everything that was good and pure and sweet back then. Nowadays you can't let your kids out of your sight, and when you want an ice cream, it costs five bucks for a cone and you're never really sure if it's actually made from milk and cream or frozen tofu and nondairy substitutes.

I was thinking about all of this the day we moved in. As we unloaded some stuff from the car, I heard a bell ringing in the distance.

"Do you hear that?" I asked my husband.

"What?" He staggered under the weight of a box of my shoes. We were supposed to just put the fragile stuff in the car, but I wanted to make sure if the moving guys we hired made off with our stuff, I still had all my footwear. I would be naked from the ankles up, but I would be well shod.

"That ringing," I said gleefully. "I think it is the Good Humor man."

"If you want some ice cream, let's get something good like Häagen-Dazs," he said.

"No! Good Humor is great!" I protested. "It is the quintessential suburban ice cream. We have to get some!"

"You will still be a suburbanite if you have Häagen-Dazs, honey. You will just be a suburbanite with better taste in ice cream and less gas."

"*Ice cream!*" shouted my son who had just gotten wind of our conversation. He knew about three words: "Mama," "Dada," and "ice cream." That's how we knew he was our son.

"If it comes down our street, we have to get some," I insisted. "It's tradition."

"Whose tradition?"

"Um. Mine," I yelled as I ran into the house to get my wallet. I was so excited. Ever since we left the city I had been feeling sad and lost. But with the arrival of the Good Humor man, I felt truly connected to the suburbs. It was like a gift from the suburban gods. I didn't need the city to fit in. I could be a suburbanite. I could do this.

I looked in my wallet and then stuck my head back out the door.

"Do you think the Good Humor man will take AmEx?"

• • •

For a week we all tried desperately to adjust to our new life. To make us feel more at home, I played an audiotape that had the sounds of police and ambulance sirens blaring, trucks backing up, and car alarms going off. It was very soothing. Then, a week after we moved to our house in the burbs, our neighbors, Garen and Sharon Van DeBeek, invited us to a barbecue at their home.

I was really excited to meet our new suburban neighbors and their friends. We had never really connected with our neighbors in the city, but that may have been because we had so little in common. Fat Tony and Mrs. Gwendylon lived in the basement apartment of the brownstone next door. I didn't call him Fat Tony because he was fat, although he was morbidly obese. *He* called himself Fat Tony and I knew this because he packed a nine-millimeter pistol tucked between the enormous folds of flab that hung over his belt and he would routinely yank the gun out and wave it around when he got drunk, yelling at passersby, "Don't mess with Fat Tony!"

Mrs. Gwendylon, his somewhat less fat wife, was a fortune-teller. She had a sign in their window that said "Mrs. Gwendylon" and she would sit at a bridge table outside their apartment with a stack of tarot cards and try to solicit business from the yuppie patrons of the cappuccino place next door.

Every night during the summer, twenty of Fat Tony's relatives would come over, they would slaughter a lamb, and then they would barbecue it on the hibachi outside on their sidewalk. It was really quite a scene. One night upon seeing this spectacle, my mother suggested that the reason they did this was because Fat Tony and his family were from the old country. I told her I thought they were probably from Queens.

Anyway, now that we were in the suburbs, I was confident that our new neighbors would be a little more like us and a little less like the characters of a Fellini movie. The husband was a doctor and his wife was a nurse, which is about as respectable as you can get in the suburbs. They had four kids, played tennis regularly, and took family vacations across the country in a tricked-out RV. They were truly suburban royalty.

Although I did *not* play tennis and got woozy at the sight of even a Band-Aid, I hoped that my former city coolness would be enough to sell me through to the suburbanites. I dragged out my cool prepregnancy clothes, thinking this would be the ideal time to impress our neighbors and their friends with my formerly hip urban-ness. I wasn't sure how impressed they would be by jeans that were so tight around my expanded post-baby backside, I looked like an overripe denim blueberry that was about to explode. But I hoped I could distract them from my lower half with a cool, oversized, tie-dyed T-shirt, some witty repartee, and fascinating tales of my previous life loaning bras to D-list celebrities. When I arrived, however, it seemed that even in my too-tight jeans and tie-dyed T-shirt, I was overdressed for the event. There were two groups of women there: One group either came directly from a tennis game or just simply dressed as though they did. They had their hair pulled back in perfect ponytails and wore cute tennis skirts with neon-colored piping and matching neon-colored socks. The other group of women wore shapeless sweatshirts and mom jeans and the must-have hair accessory for the well-dressed suburban mom: a scrunchie. Glancing back and forth between the tennis skirts and the hair scrunchies, I decided the lesser of the two evils was the scrunchies. I didn't want to take the chance that the tennis skirts would find out I hadn't played tennis since I was a kid at summer camp and then spread it around town that I was a suburban imposter.

As I approached the table of scrunchie women, I overheard them talking animatedly about another woman. While I hovered nearby, they detailed the misfortunes of a woman they all knew who was suffering from some terrible, undiagnosed disease, had several miscarriages, was on her third marriage, and had just been arrested for kidnapping. I was horrified listening to this and, unable to contain my curiosity, I finally interrupted the conversation.

"This is terrible," I blurted out. "Who are you talking about? Is this a friend of yours?"

"No," said one woman quite seriously. "It's Nicole from *Days of Our Lives.*"

After I scooped my jaw back up off the patio, I found my husband, tugged on his shirt, and whispered in his ear, "We. Have. Made. A. Terrible. Mistake."

. . .

When we lived in New York City, I could still pretend I was a cool mom, even without the job title, the paycheck, and the ability to fit into my cool clothes. However, once we moved to the burbs, there was nothing left to define me other than motherhood. Not that this wasn't an impressive job title. Just the fact that I made it through thirty-six hours of labor without doing or saying something that would result in divorce or my arrest for spousal manslaughter was an achievement unto itself. But the move to the suburbs left me without a cool leg to stand on. I mean, really, how cool could you be driving a used, maroon Buick sedan to Costco to buy a thousand-roll box of toilet paper because you now have room in your suburban house to store a thousand rolls of toilet paper. I suppose this might actually be cool if anyone in the world cared to know this useless piece of information when you're at a cocktail party with people who don't have room to store toilet paper because they still live in New York City. I realized that not having any storage space in New York City was one of those things people who live in the city complain about, but are actually secretly proud of. It's like the ultimate badge of city coolness. If you have space to store stuff, you obviously must live in an outer borough.

So now I was in the suburbs and I had to figure out how to find my inner cool without a cool job, cool clothes, and a cool car to do the work for me. This might have been my top priority, had it not been for the house, the one-year-old, and the obscene amount of laundry I was now responsible for. Somehow my days became all about putting away toys and getting my family's whites their brightest white without burning holes in their clothes with too much bleach while I fed, cleaned, and entertained my child. This didn't leave a lot of time for working on my suburban cool. The good news was that I was so busy and so tired that soon I started to forget about being cool. It became one of those hazy memories like how I used to have a waistline and real ankles and a hairstyle that cost me a month's salary to maintain.

Contrary to what I had expected, my biggest challenge when we moved was not reclaiming my coolness or figuring out how to unclog the one lone toilet in our house before someone had to use it again. It was relearning how to drive. I did actually have a license and had done a fair amount of driving, and done it well, before I moved to the city. But once I was in the city, I didn't sit behind a steering wheel again for about ten years. Not to say I was rusty or anything, but in my first month driving in the suburbs, I backed into a fence, ran over two shrubs, and lost my entire front bumper in a snowbank. Every time I would hit something, I would shrug nervously, turn to Josh in the backseat, and say, "Oops. Mommy went *blammo*. Don't tell Daddy." Not that Daddy would fail to spot a missing front bumper anyway, but one could hope.

Fortunately, I never actually hit a living person and we only had one car for me to damage. Unfortunately, that car routinely looked like an elephant sat on it. Our car was actually a hand-me-down from my parents when they moved to Florida and decided they didn't need a big, hulking maroon sedan that looked like a bloated rowboat with a roof rack. It was not a sexy vehicle by any stretch of the imagination and was only slightly cooler than having a minivan, so the fact that it looked like an elephant sat on it may have actually improved its appearance.

Because he had been a city baby and because we had no car, my son had spent very little time driving around and was not a big fan of the experience. You'd think that someone who had been so attached to his car seat that he slept in it in the crib until he was four months old would have been pretty amenable to riding in a car. But he hated it and cried every time I put him in. I liked to think that it was because it was new and unfamiliar to him, not because I drove like a drunk redneck in a monster truck rally. Regardless of the reason, he screamed like a banshee every time he got in the car and the only way I could get him to settle down was to distract him with Cheerios. This worked great until the day he gagged on a Cheerio and threw up his entire lunch all over the faux-sueded car upholstery. Then we had a bloated, maroon rowboat with a roof rack that looked like an elephant sat on it and smelled like vomit.

Fortunately, I picked up the technical aspects of driving again pretty quickly and my rate of hitting other people's garbage pails went from once a week to once a month. But accustomed as I was to the various challenges of life in the city, nothing prepared me for the experience of fighting with someone over a parking spot in the burbs. People in the suburbs are cutthroat when it comes to scoring a parking spot. The first time I drove to the mall, I went head-to-head with another driver over a spot near the entrance. There was much yelling and obscene gesturing and cursing on both sides. I finally let her have the spot because I wanted to be the bigger person and set a good example for my son. Also, she was about ninety years old and it was a handicapped spot and she had a permit and I didn't.

After several months, my son started to get the idea that our new life was going to include frequent trips in the pukeysmelling car with his mom yelling at other people in their cars and he settled down. I started to get the hang of driving and parking without needing to call AAA to tow me home. And we all accepted the fact that one day we would have a new car that would not be maroon, bloated, dented, and stinky . . . but that day was a ways off.

Never having had a car in the city, one could understand my difficulty adjusting to the driving way of life in the burbs. However, my prior city existence did *not* explain my trouble with household appliances. Like most city dwellers, we had the usual collection of appliances in our apartment and I was able to use them with a certain amount of skill and expertise, to the extent that one needs to be an expert to operate a coffeemaker. The problem was not in operating the appliances, though; it was in fixing them when they broke. When you live in a rental apartment, there is a guy known as "the super," whose sole job is to come fix things in your apartment that you and your sorry-excuse-for-a-handyman-husband can't figure out. So impressed was I by the super's skills that it was years before I realized that super stood for superintendent, not Superman. Sadly, out in the burbs, I quickly realized there is no super. Not that he was an asset in this area, anyway, but most of the time when something broke, there was no husband to help, either. Most of the time, when something broke, he was conveniently out of town on a business trip, or merely in the city at his job. I came to learn later that there is actually a universal law for this. It is called the Law of Diminishing Appliances. It says that "a household appliance will always break down, flood, short out, or die the minute your husband leaves the house." This same law, by the way, applies to your kids getting sick and the dog puking on the rug.

Now, just to recap, I have worked as a television writer and producer, delivered singing telegrams in a gorilla suit, been a waitress, and most recently, a humor columnist. None of those jobs required any knowledge of dishwasher, washing machine, or refrigerator repair. Of course, my husband has had no formal training in these areas, either. But as a man, he is supposedly hardwired to deal with these things, the same way he knows instinctively how to program the DVR and burn things on the grill. I, on the other hand, am hardwired to look at flashing, blinking lights on machines that are not working, throw up my hands in defeat, and go out to get a latte. Ergo, you can see how the Law of Diminishing Appliances, coupled with my innate inability to deal with household emergencies, can result in the fall of modern civilization in general, and my failure to get the laundry done, specifically. I actually did a pretty formidable job of handling the first couple of appliance crises that befell our house. When the dishwasher flooded the kitchen, I located the errant Power Ranger action figure that blocked the drain. And when the toaster oven ignited, I singlehandedly threw it out, went to Bed Bath & Beyond, and bought a new one.

I was starting to get a little cocky about my imaginary appliance skills, so one night after a drippy steak bathed the inside of my oven in teriyaki sauce, I decided to try using the self-cleaning function.

I'm not the most particular of housekeepers, but the one thing that I am fastidious about is the inside of the oven. I don't know why I was okay with having the inside of my car look like a garbage dump and having my son crawl around on a rug that routinely looked like ground zero of an explosion at the Frito-Lay factory, but I was not happy unless the walls of my oven shined like the day it came off the warehouse floor.

This being the case, I was overjoyed when I discovered a little button on the oven that said "self-clean." Gone were the days of wearing a gas mask while the spray-on oven cleaner filled the house with toxic fumes and punched holes in my lungs. Into the trash went the rubber gloves and radiation suit I had to wear while I scoured the glued-on pesto marinade from the oven racks. I was freed from oven-cleaning purgatory.

Since the oven came with the rental house, naturally there was no instruction manual or directions of any kind for using the self-cleaning function. There was only one button marked "self-clean," but I figured, how hard could it be? I pushed the button and left the room.

In the beginning of the cycle, everything seemed to be going along swimmingly. The oven clicked and purred. The lights flashed "Cleaning On." With my free time, I brewed a lovely cup of coffee to enjoy while my son watched a singing purple dinosaur on TV and the stove cleaned itself. But soon I noticed that the house had become a little murky. The smell of smoked meat started to waft through the house and then, suddenly, clouds of smoke billowed from the sides of the oven door and all the smoke alarms in the house went off.

"Fi-yah!" yelled my son, as he had been instructed by the singing dinosaur.

"It's not a fire," I assured him as I picked him up and moved him outside the screen door of the smoking house. "Mommy's oven is just mad."

I grabbed a broom and knocked all the smoke alarms off the ceiling, and then ran around opening every window and door in the house.

Then I went to the oven and hit "cancel." The flashing light changed from "cleaning" to "locked."

"Locked? Are you kidding me," I yelled at the oven. I was at the mercy of the self-cleaning function. I kicked the oven and yelped in pain. Now I had smoke inhalation *and* a broken toe. Cursing and hopping, I went to the back door to get some fresh air.

My son stood outside the back door screen peering in at the smoky house and the crazy oven-cleaning lady.

"You can come back in," I assured him. "It's safe."

He shook his head.

"Yucky," he said, pinching his nose.

It *was* yucky. The house was cloudy with teriyaki-laced smoke. Everything smelled like meat. But at least my oven would be clean.

When the cycle was finally finished, I threw open the oven door and looked inside.

Except for a small pile of ash on the floor of the oven, all of the teriyaki remained, and was now charred and welded to the walls. I tentatively took a sponge to it, hoping it would just slough off. It didn't budge. I slammed the oven door shut.

Sweating, smoky, and limping, I emerged from the kitchen.

"Let's not mention this to Daddy, okay?" I suggested to my son.

He looked at me and narrowed his eyes.

"Blammo."

Chapter 7

Making Friends with the Aliens in the Burbs

When I pictured my life in the burbs, I imagined a blissful existence hanging out with like-minded moms, and raising my children on Mozart and organic food I grew in the garden of a huge house with a picket fence and a big backyard. In case you are not sure, this is what professionals in the psychiatric field call Delusional Suburbanite Thinking and has no basis in reality. The main problem with my plan had to do with my exceptional powers of fertility. We had intended to wait until we were settled into the suburbs, my son was potty trained, and I had stopped driving into snowbanks before having our next child. But pretty much the minute we landed in the suburbs, I got pregnant again. This was not altogether unexpected since all I really needed to do to get pregnant was throw my underwear in a drawer with my husband's. However, it did happen quite a bit sooner than we had meant it to and I was more than a little surprised when I suddenly started throwing up again and realized it didn't have to do with drinking too much tequila or poisoning myself with my own cooking. On the one hand, I was overjoyed because it meant I didn't have to worry about losing the weight I was still carrying from the first pregnancy. However, the ensuing morning sickness that lasted nine months rendered the whole Mozart and organic food concept for baby number one, null and void.

Unlike my first pregnancy when I could just lie on the couch in my office, pretend I was working, and wallow in nauseous self-pity, the second time around I didn't have the luxury of putting my own ickiness first. Now I had a toddler to take care of and entertain, regardless of how big, fat, and pukey I was. These were certainly not the best circumstances for making new friends and I did not feel like a social butterfly at all—more like a big, fat, antisocial caterpillar.

I had thought the suburbs would be teeming with cool moms and all I'd have to do was go hang out in the playgrounds and sandboxes to meet people. While this was true to an extent, it seemed all the moms there were already friends with other moms and were not in the market for new acquaintances—especially those who were green with nausea and blown up like a frightened pufferfish. Not surprisingly, my son seemed to have a much easier time of it, and happily played with every other toddler who joined him in the sandbox. I was envious of his ability to make friends so easily and wished all it took for me to connect with some other moms was a shared joy of sand down our pants.

When the weather started to get too cold for playgrounds, I signed us up for a bunch of mommy/toddler classes at our local YMCA. I figured it would make my son happy, possibly help me meet some other moms, and at the very least, give me some new and interesting bathrooms to throw up in.

The first class we tried was something called Hands On! The class description said it was "a fun opportunity for your toddler to explore a number of different media and stimulate vital tactile learning through social interaction." I had no idea what this meant, but I saw that it involved finger paints, Play-Doh, and sand, and someone else had to clean up the mess, so I was in.

Because this was a group of toddlers, however, it was soon apparent that the class was really about snorting finger paint, ingesting Play-Doh, and dumping sand in your neighbor's hair. I realized that even though the room would be cleaned by someone else, the cleanup of my son was all on me . . . and getting hardened finger paint, wet sand, and dried Play-Doh out of every orifice of your child's body is a real drag. Moreover, I quickly learned that communal finger paint, Play-Doh, wet sand, and some weird stuff that was a mixture of cornstarch and water called "uckick" (which clearly had been named by a preschooler) are perfect transfer agents for germs carried by the free-flowing snot that seemed to be in great abundance in the class.

Not surprisingly, within a week of being Hands On!, my son had a monster head cold. Within a week and a half, I had it, too. Two colds, one nasty rash, and one stomach virus later, I finally realized that this was surely the class from hell. Additionally, with both of us getting sick every other week, I never had the opportunity to get to know the other moms in the class. By the fourth week when my son came down with a case of something truly revolting called Coxsackie virus, I didn't care how vital tactile learning was to his success in life—we were out of there.

Next on the Mommy-and-me agenda was a toddler gymnastics class. I had been a little apprehensive about this one
because I had such bad memories from my own gym days.
Back when I was in grade school and dinosaurs roamed the
Earth, the teachers had graded on ability, rather than enthusiasm and improvement. For someone who routinely tripped
up the stairs and fell over her own feet, this was not a place
where I could likely excel. The teachers made no bones about
the fact that they would give As to the girls who could do
backward somersault dismounts off the balance beam, but not
to the ones who sprained their ankles just trying to climb onto
the damn thing. The only bright spot in an otherwise torturous
decade of phys ed was the day I lost my grip on the rope climb
and landed on the gym teacher below.

With this personal history, you could understand my hesitation to voluntarily sign my son up for a gym class. However,
toddler gymnastics is a vastly different concept than grade
school phys ed. Here they played happy music, rolled on
rainbow-colored mats, and sat under giant parachutes while
the mommies flapped them over their kids' heads. Unfortunately, though, there was an issue with this class, too. But it
was not with the kids. It was with the moms.

Upon entering the room on the first day, I couldn't help
but notice that everyone in the class was:

(a) blonde,

(b) with nice little ponytails,

(c) and lovely, preppy, pink-and-green outfits that
    matched their toddlers' cute little pink-and-green
    outfits.

(d) Plus, if they were pregnant, they had cute little basketball-sized tummies under their cute little pink-and-green outfits.

My son ran in and joined in the fray while I stood in the doorway and stared. The class description had said this was an hour of fun and fitness for active toddlers. There was nothing in the brochure that indicated it was a class for suburban Stepford moms.

To be fair, I don't personally have anything against blondes with ponytails in pink and green. It just didn't seem likely that we would have much in common. I was:

(a) brunette,

(b) with medium-ish hair that was too short to fit in a ponytail,

(c) and the only thing I owned that was pink and green was a bottle of Pepto-Bismol that was past its "use by" date.

(d) However, my cute little pregnant belly was also the size of a basketball. But so were my boobs and my butt.

Still, I was willing to give the pink-and-green moms a chance because my mother always said you shouldn't judge a book by its cover, even if the book looked like a Barbie doll.

As the kids rolled happily on the rainbow mats, I spotted a couple of moms who were deep in conversation. Whatever they were discussing seemed pretty important because they looked very animated and engaged in the topic. Despite the matching blonde ponytails bobbing in sync, I was optimistic that I had found some potential friends. Forgetting my previous barbecue conversation experience, I inched my way toward the women and listened.

"Did you hear about these amazing new cleaning products?" asked Mom #1.

"No. What are they?" responded Mom #2 enthusiastically.

"They are these wipes that are pretreated with a cleaning solution so you don't have to walk around with a roll of paper towels *and* a spray bottle," said Mom #1. "They are *all in one*!!"

"No *way!*" exclaimed Mom #2 with appalling overenthusiasm.

"*Way!*" exclaimed Mom #1. "They are soooo great!"

"Wow, what a brilliant concept!" said Mom #2. Mom #1 vigorously nodded her head up and down in agreement. While they continued to extol the virtues of these amazing cleaning wipes, I suddenly became aware of a strange sound. I was pretty sure it was the last gasps of my brain cells dying.

". . . And they work just about anywhere," continued Mom #1. "You can use them on *all* your countertops and surfaces!"

"Well, I certainly hope you have some of them with you today," I added earnestly. "Because you're going to need them to clean my brains up off the floor when my head explodes from this inane conversation."

I smiled politely and moved over to stand next to the one other mom in the class I had just noticed who had short brown hair and a puss on her face. We sniffed each other like dogs in the park.

"Hi, I'm Tracy," I said tentatively. "What do you think of conversations about cleaning products?"

"Makes me want to shoot myself with a high-powered stun gun," she responded.

"Cool. Wanna get some coffee?"

. . .

"So . . . I made a friend in Gymboree," I confided to my husband in bed several weeks later.

"That's really great, honey," he enthused. "Are you guys going to hold hands at recess and tell each other secrets and stuff?"

"Hey, it was a big deal for me," I said, shoving his face into the pillow. "We've been out here for six months and this was the first mom I've met who didn't think that diaper rash treatments are the basis for interesting conversation."

"Come on," he argued. "I have a hard time believing you have only met one smart, interesting, sophisticated woman since we moved here."

"Well, I did meet one other. But right after we became friends she decided it was too stressful being home with her kids full-time and she went back to work."

"What does she do?" he asked.

"Defuse bombs."

"Ahhh," he said, nodding in understanding. He waited a moment to ensure that the conversation was over and then went back to reading his magazine.

"Unfortunately, it didn't work out," I continued.

"What didn't work out?"

"My new friend from Gymboree."

"How come?" he asked without glancing up.

"Well, we started getting friendly, and then I ran into

her at the shoe store and she was there with her husband and kids."

"And . . ."

"And she introduced me to her husband, but I realized I already knew him."

"You knew her husband?" repeated my husband, putting down the magazine again. He was suddenly a little more interested in the conversation.

"Yes, we dated in college."

"Oh. Oh!" he whispered. "When you say 'dated,' you mean . . ."

"Yeah. I mean, no, I didn't. I mean, we didn't. But she thought I did, too, and, well, she dropped out of the class and isn't returning my phone calls."

"You slut."

"Not funny."

"Sorry," he said, turning back to his magazine. "So, make some other friends, you know, with some women whose husbands you haven't slept with."

I whacked him. "It's not so easy."

"Yeah, it is," he argued.

I stared at him. "I think you think I'm a snob."

"No. I just think that maybe you have unrealistically high standards."

"That is the definition of a snob."

"Okay. Then you're a snob."

"I'm not a snob!!" I protested.

"Okay. You're not a snob."

"You're not being helpful."

He got up on one elbow and faced me. "What do you want from me, honey?" He sighed.

"I don't know," I said and suddenly choked up. I had just passed the first trimester of my second pregnancy and was only nauseous about twenty-two out of twenty-four hours of the day, which was a big improvement over the first twelve weeks, but still pretty lousy. Additionally, while I knew I was pregnant and my husband knew I was pregnant, to the outside world I just looked fat, which made me feel really crummy about myself. My boobs were bigger than watermelons, I was perpetually exhausted, had constant greasy meat cravings, hated songs that were sung by purple dinosaurs, cried whenever I saw a Disney movie where the mother died, missed eating sushi, and could not, for the life of me, understand why I was having such a hard time connecting with other moms.

"I guess I want just a little more 'Rah-rah, go, honey, you're awesome.'"

"You want a cheerleader?"

"Yes. I do. I want someone to cheer me on 'cuz I am too nauseous to cheer myself on."

"I can do that," he said and gave me a reassuring kiss on the cheek.

"And I also want a cheeseburger with pickles and olives."

"Do we have any ground beef?" he asked, dutifully getting out of bed.

I smiled wanly. "Ten pounds of it."

•   •   •

While my husband went to cook me up another Pregnant Patty Special, as we came to call them, I lay in bed and tried to figure out why I felt so disconnected since we had moved to the burbs. True, it's a challenge to make friends when you feel like you're going to throw up all the time, but I was pretty sure it was more than that. I guess part of it was I was surprised I didn't instantly bond with every other mom who had a toddler and had quit her job to stay home and raise her family. I had somewhat naively assumed that since we had that in common, we would be insta-friends, like some kind of sorority of former working girls bonded through childbirth and stretch marks. I failed to take into account that we were all different people before we'd had kids, so the act of birthing children wouldn't mean we would all automatically like each other afterward. Women who were annoying, narcissistic, shallow, or just plain boring before they had kids were still that way after they had them. The only difference was now they were all that and tired, too.

I realized I might have gone into this process backward. Rather than trying to pick up friends at toddler classes where the only thing we had in common was our kids, maybe I should have been focused on doing things where I would meet like-minded women who also *happened* to have kids. Unfortunately, with a toddler and another baby on the way, it was hard to find the time for things like book clubs or film courses where I could meet women who had more scintillating interests than diaper rashes and cleaning wipes.

As the smell of cooking hamburger meat wafted up to me, I was suddenly nauseated again and realized that while it was great to have some insight into my situation, it was likely that I was going to have to put Operation Find a Friend on hold until I could at least start a conversation with someone without puking.

Chapter 8

It's a Suburban Jungle Out There

Having a baby in the suburbs is a slightly different experience than having a baby in the city. When I went into labor in the city, we took a cab to the hospital, and then had to get out and walk the last block because the road was flooded from a water main break. When we finally got to the emergency room, I was admitted at the same time as a gunshot victim. Even though I was screaming louder, they took him first since I was only two centimeters dilated.

Two years later when I went into labor in the burbs, the hospital staff met me at the front door with a wheelchair, valet parked our car, and offered me a cappuccino on the way up to delivery. The only drama with that birth was the fact that our doctor almost missed it because he was flipping burgers at a Fourth of July barbecue.

In the doctor's defense, my daughter did come into the

world pretty fast and it *was* a national holiday so he had a good reason to be at a barbecue. The bigger issue, though, was that it seemed *every* doctor on call that day was at a Fourth of July barbecue. This left one agitated nurse and one frantic anesthesiologist to deal with a sudden onslaught of moms giving birth on Independence Day. By the time the anesthesiologist got to me and gave me my epidural, my daughter was already on her way out. Having had one kid while being loaded up on lots of drugs and one kid with absolutely nothing, I can tell you with good authority that natural childbirth sucks and those people who tell you to breathe through the pain can bite me.

Since I had already logged two years as a professional mother, I thought I had the parenting thing down pat and it would be no big deal to add one more kid into the mix. I recalled someone once saying that when you have one kid, it feels like one kid, but when you have two, it's like having two hundred. I scoffed at this when I heard it, but when my second child arrived I suddenly understood the difference. I know all the moms with four or five kids are going to think I'm a big weenie, but having two kids under the age of two was not just hard; it was so hard, so demanding, so completely overwhelming and bone-achingly exhausting that I really questioned my ability to live through that period of my life without becoming one of those pathetic moms who are so tired they start snorting hot cocoa mix.

I was prepared for the sleepless nights, the constant need for attention from my two-year-old, and the effort of carrying around size H-cup boobs again. What I was not prepared for was a newborn that suddenly stopped breathing three days after she was born.

It happened when I was feeding her. As she was nursing, I looked down, and with total horror, I noticed that she was turning blue. Instinctively I pulled her away from me and whacked her on the back. She took a big gulp of air and started to cry. So did I.

Babies turn all kinds of weird colors when they are newborns, make strange noises, and pass disgusting things from all openings of their body, but I knew that what had just happened was definitely outside the norm of reasonable and customary. Frantically, I picked up the phone and called my husband.

"I was just feeding Emily and she turned blue," I whispered urgently. My son was occupied with *Teletubbies*, but I still tried to keep my voice down so he wouldn't get scared.

"What do you mean she turned blue? Is she cold?" he asked.

"No, blue, like stopped-breathing blue."

"Oh shit. Call the doctor."

"Maybe it was just like a hiccup or something?" I suggested. Suddenly I wasn't so sure if it was as bad as I'd thought. Maybe I was blowing it out of proportion because I had just given birth three days earlier and my brain was still in shock.

"Honey, call the doctor right now!!" he repeated, more urgently.

Hesitantly, I called our pediatrician. I could tell from the tone of his normally cheerful voice that he didn't think I was blowing anything out of proportion. He told me to meet him at the neonatal unit of our hospital right away.

The kid watching *Teletubbies* was not happy to be dragged away from the TV and the kid who had been nursing was not happy to be swaddled and stuck in a car seat before mealtime was over. I threw on whatever clothes would fit over my bloated post-pregnancy body, and strapped two wailing kids into the car. At this point I was crying pretty freely, too. So with all three of us sobbing, I drove to the hospital.

. . .

"Your daughter has severe gastroesophageal reflux. Her lower esophagus sphincter, which normally prevents acid and other stomach contents from backing up into the esophagus, is premature and not fully developed so the food and stomach acid flows backward," explained the doctor to me for a second time. The first time, she used so much medical jargon I had no idea what she was saying so I asked her to explain it again in English. I'm sure part of my problem was that I was exhausted. It had been twenty-four hours since we had entered the hospital and they had inserted a pH probe into my daughter's stomach to figure out what was going on.

"When the contents of her stomach come back up, it starts to spill over into her trachea and she is at risk for gastric aspiration. This seems to be happening for up to two hours after she eats, even while she is sleeping."

I blanched. I got the gist of what the doctor was saying and it freaked me out. I grabbed my husband's arm a little tighter.

"I don't understand," I argued. "She was full term. How can she have a premature digestive system?"

"Just because we come out at forty-two weeks doesn't mean we are fully cooked," the doctor explained, comparing pregnancy to a Perdue Oven Stuffer Roaster. "We like to call the first three months of the baby's life the fourth trimester because so many of their basic systems are still developing."

"So does that mean she will outgrow this?" asked my husband.

"Definitely," she said, reassuringly. "But it could take up to six months or more. In the meantime we want to put her on two medications to make her more comfortable, help the food digest more quickly, and stop it from backing up."

"Okay," we agreed.

"And we need to put her on an apnea monitor," she added. "Babies with reflux are at a much higher risk for SIDS."

My husband and I looked at each other. When the doctor had mentioned that it could happen while the baby was sleeping, I kind of knew where she was headed. But when she actually said the word "SIDS"—sudden infant death syndrome—it seemed like all the air got sucked out of the room. Suddenly I felt like I was the one who was having trouble breathing. I grabbed my husband's arm a little tighter and inhaled deeply as the doctor gestured to a nearby table that had a machine the size of a large box of cereal resting on it. There were several knobs and buttons on the face of it and a slew of wires with electrodes attached. It looked like something Dr. Frankenstein would use to bring his creation to life.

"This is an apnea monitor," said the doctor. "Your baby will be attached to this twenty-four hours a day, except when you are bathing her. It will monitor her respiration and heart rate and a loud beep will go off if she stops breathing for more than fifteen seconds. This way you will know if she has stopped breathing while you are sleeping and you can administer CPR if necessary. Obviously you and your other caregivers will need to be trained in CPR."

I felt my knees begin to buckle.

"I need to sit down," I said to my husband. I must have looked like hell because he gave me the concerned look of someone whose partner looks like hell.

He walked me over to a chair while the doctor went to get me some water. Then he kneeled down next to me.

"It's okay," he reassured me. I could feel the tears start to burn my eyes again. He took my hand and held it hard. "First of all, this is a lot for anyone to take in, much less someone who just gave birth five days ago. The good news is, she is fine, we will know instantly if she is *not* fine, and most importantly, she will outgrow this."

I nodded but couldn't speak.

"It's just going to be a little more complicated for a while."

"Really complicated," I finally said hoarsely.

"Yes," he agreed.

"And she's going to look like a Frankenbaby," I said, staring at the apnea monitor.

He smiled. "Yes, she will be a Frankenbaby. But with you for a mother, I'm sure she will be the coolest Frankenbaby on the block."

I looked down at my oversized sweatpants and breast milk–stained maternity blouse and shook my head.

"No doubt."

. . .

Here's what they don't tell you in Apnea Monitor School: The wires and electrodes that are attached to your baby are so supersensitive that every time she so much as wiggles a toe in the middle of the night, the alarm will go off. For us, this amounted to about ten false alarms each night. The good news was there were no real alarms because the medication she was on worked so well. The bad news was the medication made her digest the food so quickly that she was hungry every two hours. This made for a particularly hairy nighttime schedule, which looked something like this:

11 p.m.: *Final bedtime feeding.*

11:30 p.m.: *Change diaper. Check apnea monitor. Put baby back to bed.*

Midnight: *False apnea alarm. Check baby. Go back to bed.*

12:30 a.m.: *False apnea alarm. Check baby. Go back to bed.*

1:00 a.m.: *1 a.m. feeding.*

1:30 a.m.: *Change diaper. Check apnea monitor. Put baby back to bed.*

2:00 a.m.: *False apnea alarm. Check baby. Go back to bed.*

2:15 a.m.: *False apnea alarm. Check baby. Go back to bed.*

2:30 a.m.: *False apnea alarm. Check baby. Go back to bed.*

3:00 a.m.: *3 a.m. feeding.*

3:30 a.m.: *Change diaper. Check apnea monitor. Put baby back to bed.*

4:00 a.m.: *False apnea alarm. Check baby. Laugh hysterically. Babble incoherently. Cry uncontrollably. Go back to bed.*

After a month of this, I was so wrung out even my fingernails hurt. By the second month I began to understand why some animals eat their young.

Although the apnea monitor was so loud I was sure it could wake Elvis from his grave, it did not seem to bother either of my kids. My son slept soundly through all the alarms and my daughter slept like, well, like a baby. I, however, was a basket case. I would fall asleep while feeding the baby, while standing at the stove stirring a pot of mac and cheese, and while sitting on the toilet. I was amazed that I managed to keep both kids alive on a daily basis, did not burn the house down, and still, somehow, continued to keep all the day-to-day things going smoothly. My daughter was the one who was attached to a machine, but I was the one who was functioning on autopilot. Although I wanted to treasure all those newborn milestones, I willed those apnea monitor days to pass as quickly as possible.

. . .

Even though I was bone tired and cringed at the thought of going anywhere with a toddler, a baby, and an apnea monitor that was so big it was like toting around a third child, I still recognized that my son needed to get out and play with other kids his age. Something told me he might be a little bitter about having a new baby around and especially one that needed so much attention. My first clue might have been the time I caught him secretly unhooking all the wires from her machine. Then there was the fact that he would smack her in the head whenever I turned away. At this point I realized he probably needed something special of his own, so I signed him up for another group play class, and the four of us (him, me, the baby, and the machine) hit the road for some much-needed social time.

The advantage of having a baby attached to a giant machine is it's a really great conversation starter. Although most of the other moms were polite enough not to ask why our baby had a bunch of wires poking out of her clothes, their kids didn't have the same inhibitions.

"Is your baby a robot?" asked one toddler.

"Does she come with batteries?" asked another.

"That's cool!" exclaimed a third. "We have a baby, too, but he just poops and cries."

"My baby is named Em-lee and this is her apnea mono-door," boasted my son, suddenly taking proud ownership of his sister and her accessories. We had explained to him in very simple terms what the monitor was and why she needed it, which is probably how he got the idea to disconnect her wires in the first place. Although he was clearly not a fan at first, he was quick to realize that when you have something everyone else wants to have, suddenly that thing becomes much more valuable. Of course, this is only true for the instant in time when the other kids are expressing interest in whatever you have. The second we got home and it was just him and his sister, he was back to whacking her whenever I wasn't looking.

But for now, he got to be the star by association. And suddenly, so was I.

"Apnea monitor?" guessed one of the other moms, plunking down next to me on the bench reserved for mommies, younger siblings, and Frankenbabies.

I nodded.

"How are you doing with it?" she asked.

"Not so bad." I shrugged, downplaying the difficulty of the

situation. "On the upside, we can use her as a generator when the power goes out."

The other mom laughed. I liked her immediately. She had brown hair, she wore all black, and she laughed at my jokes. What more could you want in a friend?

"She also makes a great cappuccino," I added.

"Does she come with a frother?"

"Sadly, no."

"Too bad." She nodded in the direction of a robust-looking, redheaded little girl who had just knocked my son down. "She was on one, too," she confessed. "For about six months I babbled incoherently and slept on the checkout line at the supermarket."

"Did you sleep standing on line or did you actually lie down on the conveyer belt?"

"Standing."

"Yeah. Me, too." We sat in compatible silence for a moment watching our kids tear around the room like a pack of crazed, sugared-up savages. The box of mini doughnuts and cider they inhaled at the start of the class might have had something to do with it.

"I'm Lori," she said, extending her hand and introducing herself.

"Tracy. Nice to meet you." I shook back. "You know, you don't sound like a Jersey girl," I blurted out.

She laughed. "Midwest. Just as bad. How about you?" she asked. I shook my head.

"No. We moved here from the city about a year ago. My husband said if we came out here, his parents would help us with the kids."

"You fell for that?"

"Yeah. It's okay." I shrugged. "I told him I wasn't going to gain any weight after we got married, so I guess we're even."

We chatted easily for several minutes until I saw my son suddenly haul off and shove her daughter hard into a ball pit. I jumped up to reprimand him, forgetting that I was holding my sleeping daughter who was still tethered to the apnea machine on the floor. The machine instantly let out a high-pitched alarm as the wires became disconnected from the baby. She got startled and started to cry, which set off two other babies in the room, as well as the girl in the ball pit. Within fifteen seconds, every kid in the room was crying and every mom was glaring at me for disrupting their hour of semi-freedom. I looked around, frozen in place by the sudden onslaught of mayhem.

My new friend got up to rescue her daughter from the depths of the ball pit, turned to me, and smiled.

"Are we having fun yet?"

* * *

Although Lori and I shared a similar distaste for blonde women who wore pink and green and spent their time discussing cleaning products and diaper wipes, unlike me, she had at least managed to find some friends in the burbs and was happy to bring me into the fold. Soon after we met, she invited me to join a playgroup. Not having participated in this ritual of new motherhood before, I wasn't sure what, if anything, I was supposed to bring. Although my mother suggested I make a brisket, I instead chose to bring three bags of leftover Halloween candy. As the bearer of large quantities of Reese's Peanut Butter Cups, I thought this would have the double benefit of endearing me to my new mommy friends while also ridding my house of the chocolate peanut butter devil that was single-handedly derailing my post-pregnancy weight-loss efforts.

While this was a good concept in theory, I neglected to take one possibility into account.

"Oh *no*!" yelled the mom who was hosting the playgroup when I dumped the candy on her table. The kids swarmed the table like locusts. She quickly scooped all the candy into a large bowl and held it over her head while shooing the kids off into another room with a bowl of pretzels.

I stood there dumbfounded. Somehow I had broken some cardinal rule of snack food protocol. I wondered if it was a city/suburb thing and maybe in the burbs you are only supposed to serve Kit Kats at playgroups. I made a mental note to curse Lori for not coaching me on proper candy etiquette.

"Is there a problem with the peanut butter cups?" I asked hesitantly.

"Jonah can't have them!" she responded with obvious exasperation about one of the kids in the playgroup. "He has *severe* peanut butter allergies. He can't even be in the room if other kids are eating it."

"I'm so sorry. I had no idea," I stammered.

"Well, maybe you should have asked before you brought something potentially *life-threatening* to someone's house," she said coldly.

"What about his school?" I asked, ignoring her tone. "What if someone brings in a peanut butter and jelly sandwich?"

"None of the kids at the school are allowed to bring *those* for lunch. It is a peanut-free preschool," she said with what I thought was a certain air of haughtiness. "*Most* moms are fine with that." She stuck the bowl of candy on top of a rack of shelves, sashayed out of the room to join the playgroup, and left me standing in the kitchen by myself.

All this time I had been afraid that people wouldn't like me for who I was. I was relieved to now know they just wouldn't like me because I was the idiot, thoughtless peanut butter mom. I felt bad but I was also annoyed. How the hell was I supposed to know there was a kid in the playgroup who was allergic to peanut butter? Is that one of the questions you're supposed to ask when you're applying for playgroup membership? If so, I guess I missed the memo.

"Hey, are you coming in?" Lori poked her head into the kitchen.

"I'm not sure I should. Apparently I violated the Suburban Peanut Butter Law and there might be a warrant out for my arrest. I wouldn't want to put the rest of you in danger for being my accomplices."

"Huh?"

"I brought Reese's Peanut Butter Cups to the playgroup," I admitted. "I don't want to be unsympathetic because I know it is a serious allergy, but Cheryl nearly bit my head off."

Lori rolled her eyes. "Forget about it. She's a pain in the ass. No one likes her but she started the group so it's hard to kick her out. Besides, she's the only one willing to let us all come here and destroy her house."

I looked around the kitchen. There wasn't a single spatula out of place. It could not have been neater if no one actually lived here. Above the sink there was a hand-painted wooden sign that said "A Clean Home Is a Happy Home." I thought it would make a nice cracking sound when I broke it over her high-and-mighty head. Lori followed my eyes to the sign and rolled her eyes.

"I'll tell you something else, but you can't say anything," she whispered.

"What?"

"Her kid isn't even allergic to peanuts. Cheryl made that up to get him into the private school she wanted him to attend that also happens to be peanut-free. He wouldn't have gotten in otherwise."

"Are you kidding me?" I gaped at her.

"Swear to God," she said, grinning.

I was appalled. "I thought parents only did that kind of stuff in the city."

She shook her head. "No, we have our crazy moms out here in the suburbs, too."

"Clearly." I looked over at the bowl of contraband peanut butter cups.

"What about the rest of them?" I wondered, gesturing to the moms in the other room. "Will they judge me for wanton peanut butter cup distribution?"

"Only if you keep them for yourself," she retorted. As we turned to leave, I grabbed a couple of handfuls of peanut butter cups from the bowls and stuffed them in my jacket pockets. Then Lori took my arm and led me into a great room stuffed with moms, babies in car seats, and toddlers climbing on and playing with every plastic toy imaginable. As the kids pulled one toy out, Cheryl scrambled down to the floor to put a discarded toy away. It was a losing battle, but it was fun to watch her try to contain the chaos.

"Hi, I'm Tracy," I said waving to the group when I entered. "I'm a stay-at-home mom and a peanut butter cup–aholic."

"Hi, Tracy!" responded the two other moms in unison. Cheryl shot me a dirty look. I plunked the Frankenbaby in her car seat down on the floor with her two-ton apnea monitor next to her and squeezed myself into a toddler chair that had the name "Jonah" painted on the seat.

As Josh ran into the fray, one of the kids with hair the same color as Cheryl's came over to me.

"Dat's my chair," he said firmly.

"Are you Jonah?" I asked him.

"Yeah."

"It's a great chair. Is it okay if I sit on it while you guys play?"

"No," he said. "You aw too fat. You gonna bwake it."

I blanched. Whether or not it was true, and it probably was, it was still harsh to hear from the mouth of a three-year-old. I looked at his mother to see if she was going to say anything, but she just raised her eyebrows, smiled, and shrugged. I could see this was going to get ugly.

"No problem." I smiled sweetly at him. "How about if I switch seats with your mommy? Can she sit in your chair?"

"No!" he stated. "She too fat, too!"

I grinned knowingly. I had figured he was an equal-opportunity insulter. This time his mother was not as understanding.

"Jonah, it's not nice to call people fat. People come in all shapes and sizes and we treat everyone nicely . . ." She nodded toward me. "No matter how big they are."

"No fat mommies in my chair!" he bellowed. He pushed

on the back of the chair with amazing strength for a three-year-old and dumped me onto the floor.

Two of the other moms burst out laughing. "Guess I better sit on the floor," one of them snorted. "I'm a fat mommy, too."

"I'm the mother of all fat mommies," said the other mom. She wasn't fat at all but small and toned with a mane of gorgeous chestnut-colored hair. I appreciated the sentiment, though.

"I'm Shari, by the way," she introduced herself.

"And I'm Becca," said the other mom sitting next to me. She was actually bigger than me, but I couldn't tell if she was still carrying around old baby weight or if she was pregnant with another one. I was firmly of the belief that you do not ask a woman if she is pregnant until you see the baby's head crowning between her legs.

Lori joined us on the floor and we all exchanged small talk while the kids did their best to dismantle Cheryl's great room. Just as I was starting to feel like I could fit in with the group, Emily started to whimper in her sleep.

"Uh-oh. That's the ten-minute warning whimper," I said. "I have to go before she wakes up."

"Can you feed her here?" asked Lori.

"Nah. It's a whole thing. I have to undo all the wires and change her and then reattach her to the machine and then feed her. It's easier at home in my Frankenbaby laboratory."

The other moms nodded in understanding. I stood up and grabbed the car seat and called Josh. Then I said my good-byes and started to leave. But halfway out the door I stopped when I remembered the candy. Reaching into my jacket pockets, I grabbed a handful of candy out and tossed them at the other moms.

"Leftover Halloween candy," I explained. "I'm sharing the calories. Eat these later when your kids aren't looking."

Cheryl glared at me from across the room and started to say something about peanuts, but I shot her my best city-girl death stare and she snapped her mouth shut.

I decided the time had come to make friends and if she didn't like my methods, she could just kiss my big, fat, peanut butter cup ass.

. . .

Two months later, the apnea doctor gave us the thumbs-up.

"We are finally done with the stupid apnea monitor," said my husband as I snuggled up to him in bed on the six-month anniversary of our trip to the neonatal ICU. "What should we do to mark the occasion?"

I kissed him passionately. "Let's have another baby."

"*What*??"

"Just kidding."

. . .

Once my daughter was off the apnea monitor, life got simpler just by virtue of the fact that I was now able to get at least several hours of uninterrupted sleep at a time, *and* I didn't have to wire my daughter up like a sound system every time we left the house. Still, I did not *feel* like I was in a better place. For some reason I felt more lost, more unsatisfied with my life, and definitely more uncool than ever before.

"I think I need a makeover," I said to my husband one day as I felt around my head and discovered a number of pieces of Pepperidge Farm Goldfish in my hair. I'm not sure how the goldfish, which were being eaten by my now-one-year-old daughter on the other side of the room, managed to get in my hair, twenty feet away, but this is the nature of motherhood. It is one of the lesser known Laws of the Universe: Anything messy and disgusting that your kids eat will be drawn across time and space, through the magnetic pull of the Earth's axis, and eventually end up all over you. This is also true of modeling clay, finger paint, and glitter.

"Which part of you do you want to make over?" he asked.

"All of me," I said, flicking off dried pieces of banana that were glued to my shirt. "I hate my hair. I hate my clothes. I used to be cool and now I'm covered with drool. And glitter." I sighed. "I need to reboot my image."

"You look like a mom," he said sweetly. I know he meant this in the most adoring and loving way. But I couldn't have been more insulted if he'd told me I looked like the leader of a polka band.

I wish I could say the problem was just the goldfish and the glitter. But they were just the final straw. I had been sliding down the uncool abyss for years, starting with pregnancy and lasting well beyond potty training (my son's, not mine). Before kids I had a cool job, a cool haircut, and cool clothes. It was a carefully cultivated image that I had worked hard to create . . . undoing the damage of years of tight Gloria Vanderbilt jeans, bowl-shaped Dorothy Hamill haircuts, and sinfully ugly Earth shoes when I was younger. I had successfully reinvented myself to be a cool city chick and now, two kids later, I was back where I started in tight mom jeans, a bowl-shaped mom haircut, and Uggs.

If I had to be really honest with myself, the mom jeans and the Uggs were the symptom. The problem was the inner me. Somewhere along the line, I had lost my identity. Sure, I was a mom, and intellectually I knew this was the hardest job I would ever have, but it was not a cocktail-party-conversation job. When my husband and I used to go out to parties before I had kids, people would ask what I do. I would say, "I work in television," and they would be very impressed, and I would be very impressed with myself, too. But when I quit my job to stay home with the kids, it was a whole different ball game. At parties when they asked what I did and I would say, "I'm a stay-at-home mom," they would say, "Ooooh, that's nice" and then their eyes would glaze over and they would go find someone else with a "real" job to talk to. They weren't impressed anymore, and I guess I wasn't so impressed, either. Instead of talking about the famous people I worked with and the exciting job I had, I had become one of those women who talked about the cute little things my kids did that day. You might argue that the people I counted on for validation were incredibly superficial, and naturally, I would agree. But it was more validation than I was getting in my current position as chief macaroni and cheese cook and sippy cup washer.

Of course my husband would constantly tell me I was doing a great job with the kids and the kids would tell me I was the world's greatest mommy, but I found it extraordinarily hard on my ego to exist in a working person's world without having a job title. For a while, I would go to parties and play the "I used to" game.

"Well, I *used to* work in television and we *used to* live in New York City," I would say, and then blurt out quickly and quietly, "But-now-I'm-home-in-the-suburbs-with-the-kids." I was embarrassed that I was embarrassed by my choices, and yet I couldn't escape the feeling that I just wasn't relevant anymore, and this made me feel even worse.

I think what happens when you feel bad about yourself internally, is it starts to play out externally. I gained weight. I let my cute little haircut grow out into a mom bob. I bought cheap jeans out of bins at Costco because the expensive department store jeans didn't look good on me anyway. I gave up on stylish but impractical shoes and surrendered to Uggs.

And I stopped talking about what I used to do.

But if I wasn't what I do, then who was I? There was a person in me who existed before I worked in television and before I got married and before I became a mother. I thought she was still in there, under the bad mom hair and the Uggs, but I had no idea who she was or what she was about. So when I said to my husband, "I need a makeover," what I really meant was, "I need to make myself over." I needed to find out who I was and then find a place where being "a mom" and being "a me" could coexist.

Chapter 9

"P" Is for Parenting and Prozac

There is almost always a defining moment when you know you've hit bottom. For some people it is that final drunken binge. For others, it is that forbidden number on the bathroom scale. For me, it was the day I got pulled over by a cop while I was driving in my bathrobe.

When you live in the city and you walk everywhere, you're forced to get up and put on actual clothes to go out. Even if you've had the night from hell, you still have to get dressed to go out, unless you are one of those crazy New Yorkers who walk through the streets in your bathrobe yelling at invisible people, or you're Hugh Hefner. But for the rest of us, life in the city is not clothing-optional.

Out in the suburbs, however, it's an entirely different scenario. There are many times when you might have to drive somewhere but never actually get out of your car. When this is the case, you realize you could really wear almost anything . . . or nothing. Of course I'm not advocating driving naked, because, clearly, it is inappropriate and can even be kind of painful if you have leather seats and it's a hot day. But, driving in your bathrobe, which essentially counts as being clothed, does not really cut it in terms of appropriate driving attire.

Needless to say, I was not always a bathrobe driver. When we first relocated, I swore I would never be one of those women who drove in anything they wouldn't be caught dead in at the mall. But it's amazing what two kids, lack of sleep, an eroding self-image, and having only one car will do to you. Since I needed the car to get around suburbia, I had to get both the kids up at the crack of dawn every day so I could drive my husband to the train. The bright side to this misery was that if I got up a little extra early, I could take a shower, get dressed in something somewhat cool, suck down a pot of coffee, and go. The advantage to this plan was that with my husband home and on kid duty for an hour, I was assured of actually getting a shower in that day, and maybe, if I was lucky, even getting a chance to be in the bathroom by myself. But after a while I realized I had become complacent about my life as a stay-at-home mom, and I started to get lazy.

At first I followed my usual routine. But soon I found myself getting up a little later, showering, doing my makeup, but foregoing the cool clothes and just throwing on some jeans and a T-shirt. Then I began waking up even later, showering, and foregoing both the makeup and the cool clothes. When even that proved too taxing, I woke up even later, skipped the shower altogether, and just threw on whatever clothes were closest to the bed or on the top of the laundry heap.

Then one day, the inevitable happened. I hit the snooze button five times, woke up five minutes before I had to drive my husband, and without a moment's hesitation, I threw on my bathrobe.

"What are you doing?" my husband asked incredulously when I appeared in the kitchen with my pocketbook, kids in hand, and my big fluffy blue bathrobe wrapped around my body.

"What do you mean, what am I doing?" I replied sleepily. "I'm driving you to the train."

"I mean, what are you doing in your bathrobe?"

"I'm driving you to the train," I repeated. I wasn't sure what the issue was here. I had my keys and license. I wasn't doing anything illegal. Stupid and incredibly unattractive, maybe. But not illegal.

"You can't drive me to the train in your bathrobe," he said. "What if someone sees you? What if you get a flat? Everyone will start calling you the Crazy Bathrobe Lady."

I looked at him wearily. The kids had taken turns waking up every hour, all night, and I was so tired even the hair follicles on my head were exhausted. Early on in the child-rearing process, my husband and I had agreed that it was my job as the stay-at-home mom to deal with these late-night interruptions so he could function at his job during the day and earn the money. One would think that I, too, would need to function during the day so I didn't fall asleep at the wheel and drive into a tree, but that is an argument I had yet to win. So for now, it was my duty to go to the kids when they woke up in the middle of the night, soothe them back to sleep, or club them over the head, whichever was more effective.

"Everyone in the suburbs drives in their bathrobes," I

argued. "Besides, I have been driving for twenty-something years and I've never gotten a flat."

He shook his head. "I think it's a bad idea," he warned. "I guarantee that the day you drive in your bathrobe is the day something will happen that you wished you hadn't driven in your bathrobe."

"Like what?" I challenged. I was feeling petulant and argumentative. Two hours of sleep will do that to you.

"I don't know. Get stopped by a cop?"

"What is he going to do?" I wondered. "Arrest me for driving in an ugly bathrobe?"

"I don't know, honey. This is the suburbs. He might. They're not used to crazy bathrobe people out here the way they are in the city."

"I'm not crazy. I just look that way," I shot back. "Now where are my bunny slippers?"

He rolled his eyes in resignation.

I guess somewhere deep in the recesses of my suburbanly transplanted brain I kind of knew I was on a slippery slope. But I am nothing if not a good rationalizer and I figured, it was only a mile to the train station and back and it was very unlikely that anything would happen. Even if it did, I'd at least get a good story out of it to tell my grandchildren one day . . . assuming I survived the suburbs and child-rearing to tell about it.

• • •

Driving my husband to the train while I was dressed in my bathrobe was such a rousing success that I decided to drive my son to preschool that way, too. Since I didn't have to get out of the car—I could just drop him off in the school circle—

no one would be the wiser. Thinking about it, I realized that I could actually get through a good chunk of my day in my bathrobe without ever leaving the car. The dry cleaners was a drive-through . . . the car wash was a drive-through . . . I could get my daughter lunch at a drive-through. If I could just figure out how to convince the supermarket to become a drive-through, there was a good chance I might never have to change out of my bathrobe again.

Unfortunately, my master bathrobe plan only lasted a whopping two days. After dropping my son off at school, I was on my way home with my daughter in the car when I saw the flashing lights in my rearview mirror. I pulled over so the cop could pass, thinking he was after some *other* delinquent mom driving in her bathrobe who had made an illegal left turn coming out of the school parking lot. When I saw the police car pull over behind me and the cop get out, I shook my head in disbelief. In what was either the desperate action of a completely delusional woman or the vain act of an almost middle-aged mom, I quickly yanked down the sun visor to check my face in the mirror. I'm not sure why I thought it was important to make sure that my face was presentable when I was driving in my bathrobe and slippers, but in the seconds while I waited for the cop to get to my car, I whipped out my lipstick and applied a fresh coat. This is kind of like putting a diamond tiara on a chimpanzee, but I thought it certainly couldn't hurt the situation.

• • •

"Excuse me," the cop said suddenly, leaving my window and turning to walk back to his car. I wondered if he was going to call this in. I suspected there was a code for this kind of thing . . . like a 10-80: Harried Mom of Two Making Illegal

Left Turn While Driving in Her Bathrobe. I was pretty sure I would get points on my license for this, or at the very least, they might take away my Neiman Marcus credit card.

I considered my options. He had not yet seen my license or registration so assuming he hadn't run my plates, I could floor it and make a run for the nearest Dunkin' Donuts and try to blend in with the other suburbanites in their bathrobes. However, if I got caught, I would certainly face even worse charges, including contributing to the delinquency of a minor (my daughter) by taking her on the lam with me (to Dunkin' Donuts) and subjecting her to possibly damaging ridicule for being seen out in public with a crazy woman in a ducky bathrobe. The other option, of course, was to throw myself on the mercy of the court and plead postpartum depression, or sleep-deprived insanity, or the Twinkie defense. Although no one in our family eats Twinkies, we do keep a box in the pantry for just such a purpose.

"Hey, sweetie, don't say anything else to the police officer, okay?" I asked my daughter over my shoulder while we waited for the return of Officer Ray-Ban. "Mommy is trying to talk her way out of a ticket."

"Wassa ticket?"

"It is something you get from a police officer when you do something wrong," I told her.

"Did you do something wrong, Mommy?" she asked.

"You mean like, in general, or just today?"

"Huh?"

"Never mind," I said. "The police officer stopped Mommy because I made a turn that I wasn't supposed to."

"Oh, I thought he stopped you because you were driving in your bathrobe like Daddy told you not to."

When the cop returned, he admonished me for making an illegal left turn, mentioned that I had a taillight out, and suggested I get a new bathrobe. He let me off with a warning, in all probability, because he was afraid if he gave me a ticket, I would show up at traffic court in my footie pajamas.

"Well, that was close," I breathed as the cop walked away to inflict pain on some other poor sleep-deprived mom. I'm pretty sure this is one of the things they cover in suburban cop school. That, and the enduring chicness of mirrored Ray-Bans.

"Did you talk your way out of the ticket, Mommy?" asked my daughter.

"Yes, I did," I gloated.

"Okay. Can we go home now 'cuz I think I peeded in my pants," admitted my daughter.

I sighed. "Me, too, sweetie."

. . .

It's amazing how a little thing like being stopped by a cop while you are driving in your bathrobe can wake you up to all that is wrong in your life. My days had been full with play-dates, toddler classes, laundry, and shopping. But without registering my vote, I realized I had settled into a world of suburban complacency. I accepted everyone else's priorities as my own and was a willing accomplice in surrendering the individuality I had placed so much value on before having kids and moving to the burbs. This is not to say I wasn't aware that something was lacking in my life. But I was reluctant to sit down and figure out what it was. I had almost convinced myself that I was completely fulfilled as a stay-at-home mom and didn't need a paycheck, a deadline, or a pat on the back to make me feel good about what I was doing. My conscious mind fell for this hook, line, and sinker. But my subconscious mind knew this was all a lot of bull doody.

I should have figured out something was up when my back started going out with alarming frequency, I had flare-ups of irritable bowel syndrome, and I started to get migraines. When I mentioned this to my friend Lori, she loaned me a book by a doctor who suggested that many mysterious back pains, headaches, and stomachaches (check, check, check) not caused by injury or illness may actually be the body's way of distracting you from negative emotions. The symptoms are psychologically generated rather than physiological in origin. The idea is that if you are busy thinking about the physical pain you are in, you won't think about your emotional pain.

After ruling out terminal brain tumors, stomach cancer, degenerative disc disease, and the possibility that aliens had kidnapped me and performed experiments on my body, I decided there might actually be some merit to the mind/body connection theory. I knew I had pain. I knew I was unhappy. Could there be a chance they were related? Connecting the dots of all my various complaints, it certainly seemed like it could be possible. It was a slow realization to take hold, but then one day as I lay on an ice pack in bed, popping ibuprofen like Skittles and willing my horrific back pain to go away so I could get up and take care of my children, I had an epiphany that maybe the back pain wasn't making me unhappy; maybe being unhappy was giving me back pain. This is what mental health professionals would call an "aha" moment, as in, "*Ah have* a feeling I should be on antidepressants."

Up until that moment, I had blamed my unhappiness on my physical discomfort, on the difficulties of parenting young children, on the extra weight I had put on with my pregnancies, and just about any other external excuse that was floating out there in the cosmos. Flat on my back with nothing to do but think about how miserable I was, I realized, suddenly, that I had to take responsibility for my own misery. And with that thought, I had hope. Because if I were responsible for my circumstances, then I could change them.

Of course change doesn't happen overnight. Experience has taught me that right after you take one step forward, you usually take two giant steps back. One of those giant steps was driving to school in my bathrobe. The other was getting stopped by a cop while driving in my bathrobe.

At this point, I was pretty sure I had hit my lowest low. I figured, it was time for a change, and if I put my mind to it, it could only get better from here.

My first call was to my former therapist. Although I hadn't gotten a lot from her when I had seen her previously, I figured the least she could do for me was recommend a psychiatrist who could write me a prescription for an antidepressant. I guess I should have been flattered that she had felt so comfortable with me that she would routinely get chemical peels and then come to our session with her face sloughing off without worrying that it might be something of a distraction for me. Still, I wasn't in therapy to make my therapist comfortable, so after the third peel, I thanked her for her help, complimented her smooth, youthful-looking skin, and left to find a new therapist. Although I heard she had stopped seeing patients and had started a new career as a physician's assistant at a plastic surgery office ("Great benefits and seventy-five percent off every cosmetic procedure!") she was still able to refer me to a psychiatrist.

. . .

"What makes you think you need to be on an antidepressant?" asked Dr. Fancypants Psychiatrist with ten diplomas on his wall. Did I care that he was also a veterinarian? No. A little concerned maybe that he might euthanize me if I peed on his rug, but no, I was not impressed by the extra degree.

"I'm depressed," I responded.

"Have you tried therapy?"

"For ten years, off and on."

"Has that helped you?"

"Yes, I learned that if you get more than two chemical peels in a year, your lips start to fall off."

"Do you ever have suicidal thoughts?" he asked.

"Suicidal? No. Murderous? Yes. Especially when my husband leaves his socks all over the house."

"Do you have any physical complaints?"

"Ever since I had kids I have started getting fat in weird places like my armpits and my earlobes," I admitted. "Oh and I've also started sprouting chin hairs."

"I mean, any physical discomfort. Headaches? Backaches? Stomachaches?"

"Yes," I said. "All of those."

"When you feel depressed are you unable to eat?"

"I wish."

He nodded and made a note next to the mass of notes he had already jotted down. He had hardly looked up as he ran through his checklist of depression questions. I wasn't sure if he thought I fell into the general depressed stay-at-home mom category or if he thought I might truly be dangerous to myself and others.

"Just in case you were wondering, I am depressed, but I am not a danger to myself or others," I clarified.

This time he looked up.

"You know, unless someone takes the last cookie I was planning to have at the end of the day as a reward to myself for keeping the kids happy, nutritionally balanced, and alive," I continued. "Then I might be a danger to whoever took the cookie, but only if that person is my husband."

"Good to know," he said, writing again.

I made a mental note going forward to only respond to questions that were asked and not volunteer any more information, lest I end up bound to a stretcher in a psych ward somewhere. We sat in strained silence for a minute while he looked over his notes and I checked out the fine collection of pharmacological encyclopedias on his bookshelf. I noticed the most recent one was dated 1979, which made me concerned that he might put me on a drug that they later discovered caused you to grow an extra liver or head.

"Well, I do think you are depressed," he finally said. "And I think you would benefit from a low-dose SSRI."

"Oh. I thought I needed an antidepressant," I said dejectedly. Apparently I was worse off than I had thought.

"SSRI stands for selective serotonin reuptake inhibitor. That is an antidepressant. Serotonin is the chemical in the brain that helps you feel good. Basically an SSRI works to prolong the action of serotonin in your brain so you feel less depressed."

"That sounds good," I said, not fully understanding what he was saying but optimistic that he knew what he was doing. "By the way, any chance this drug has magic weight-loss properties, too?"

"No. Actually, some people have experienced weight gain with these drugs."

I rolled my eyes. I knew there was a catch. If there were going to be undesirable side effects, I would have preferred the medicine caused me to grow a mustache, which I could just wax off, rather than gain weight, which is much harder to lose quickly without a lap band or lipo. So the choice was I could either be happy and fat or unhappy and thin. However since I was currently unhappy and fat, I figured I stood a better chance of being motivated to diet and exercise if I was happy and fat than unhappy and fat. What it came down to though, really, was that my kids didn't need a thin mommy; they needed a happy one. If I had to take one pound for the team, or ten, to give my kids a better, happier mom, then so be it. And while it was partly about them, it was mostly about getting myself to a place where I could begin the process of rediscovering who I was and who I wanted to be.

Part Two

The robe to success is always under construction.

—Not quite Lily Tomlin

Chapter 10

I Don't Mind Living Out of a Box as Long as There's More Than One Bathroom

One of the interesting things about kids is that they almost always need to go to the bathroom at the *exact* moment that you are in the bathroom yourself. It's like some kind of human telepathic bathroom connection. No sooner will I sit to do my business than one of the kids will urgently break into the bathroom announcing they need to go *now*! Since two out of the four of us were relatively new to this concept of holding it in for a minute, it was usually in my best interest to defer to those members of the family who were under three feet tall, grabbing their crotch, and hopping up and down in an unmistakable bladder-challenged dance, lest I find myself cleaning up a puddle on the bathroom floor and doing another load of laundry.

Mornings were even harrier when I was in the shower, my husband was at the sink shaving, my son was on the toilet, and my daughter was on the potty. Four people in a bathroom is tough. Four people in a bathroom the size of a broom closet is a clown car. I decided Walt Disney was right: It was a small world after all. Especially in my house.

Soon it became clear that one bathroom just wasn't going to cut it anymore. The writing was on the wall the day that the lone toilet broke and we were all forced to use my daughter's potty.

"I have some bad news," I said to my husband when I called him at work later that day.

I heard a sharp intake of breath. "You're not pregnant again, are you?"

I sighed. "Am I vomiting?"

"No."

"Then I'm not pregnant."

He sounded relieved. We were just starting to come out of those obscenely sleep-deprived years and could see the light at the end of the Thomas the Tank Engine tunnel. We had gone into our marriage naively thinking we would have three or maybe even four kids. But after one colic baby, two pukey pregnancies, and the *Apnea Monitor Nightmare from Hell*, as we will always fondly remember it, neither one of us was on board with the idea of more children. The kids also seemed content to keep our family at four. Actually, my son would have been happy to keep our family at three. This was clear to me when he pushed his toddler sister into a wall, requiring a trip to the emergency room and three stitches to her forehead. She got even some years later when a well-placed foot sent him flying face-first onto the playground gravel. Then it was his turn at the emergency room to get a glob of medical glue to close up his chin.

It's always so rewarding as a parent when your kids love each other like ours do.

"The bad news is the toilet died and the potty broke," I informed him.

"Come again?"

"This morning the potty broke when someone who weighs far too much to be using a plastic potty as a step stool stood on it and smashed it to smithereens."

"Who would that be?" he asked.

"I don't know, but if you find the bitch, tell her I want my old body back."

"Anyway," I continued, "I had to stand on the potty to reach the smoke alarm."

"Why were you trying to reach the smoke alarm?" he inquired reluctantly.

"'Cuz it was going off."

"And the smoke alarm was going off why?"

I wondered if I should lie, tell the truth, or pretend the phone suddenly died.

"Honey, why was the smoke alarm going off?" he repeated. "Did you use the self-cleaning function in the oven again?"

"No. And that's a misnomer. It's a self-dirtying and self-smoking function."

"Then why did the smoke alarm go off?"

"Because the Shrinky Dinks caught fire in the oven."

I waited for him to mentally catch up. I looked at my fingernails. I definitely needed a manicure. Maybe a paraffin treatment. Quite possibly, electroshock therapy, as well.

"So let me recap," he started. "The Shrinky Dinks caught fire, which made the smoke alarm go off so you stood on the kids' potty to reach the smoke alarm and the potty broke."

"Yes!" I exclaimed.

"So, how did the toilet break?" he asked.

"The sink was full of dishes and I didn't want to put a tray of burning Shrinky Dinks in there so I threw them in the toilet."

I waited for his response. When none came, I continued.

"I meant to fish them out later, but I forgot and one of the kids went to the bathroom and flushed the toilet, which you know they *never* do, and the toilet overflowed and died." I took a deep breath. "So now we have to move because we literally do not have a pot to piss in."

He sighed. I knew he thought I had orchestrated this whole scenario because I really did want to move, but honestly, I'm just not that conniving. Well, actually, yes, I am that conniving. But in this case, I really did not plan the untimely death of our toilet and half toilet.

The truth was, it was not just the bathroom that was an issue. The kids each had their own tiny room, but my husband and I were living in the attic and the basement kept flooding and there was no playroom and no storage. We had definitely outgrown our space. And since it was a rental, there was no option to add on or knock down.

We had always known that the house would be a transitional place, and with my son starting kindergarten soon, it seemed like the right time to put down some permanent roots somewhere . . . hopefully in a place with multiple bathrooms, lots of closets, and an oven that could withstand the rigors of cooking Shrinky Dinks. Wanting a bigger place and being able to afford a bigger place, however, are two different issues. Since we had rented an apartment, and then rented a house, we still had no equity and very little savings. I offered to sleep with a rich guy for a million dollars, like Demi Moore did with Robert Redford in *Indecent Proposal*, but there were multiple problems with this plan. First of all I looked nothing like Demi Moore, even when she was pregnant. Second, and perhaps more important, there were no rich guys offering. Fortunately my husband had a new job prospect on the horizon that would help us make a down payment on a modest upgrade and would save me from entering the seedy world of suburban prostitution.

Ultimately, the problem in finding a house was not so much the money, but *someone's* unrealistic expectations that we could find a big house with a big yard on a quiet street in a nice town with good schools, a train station, nice people, nice parks, good shopping, *and* a few other Jews around so our kids would not be the only ones making menorahs in art class at Christmastime.

After four months of looking, though, it became clear that the only place where all this existed was in my mind.

"We have to compromise on some of these things," said my husband after another frustrating weekend of looking at tiny houses in nice towns and big houses in icky towns.

I agreed. "Okay. Forget the Jews."

The other thing working against us was that we happened to pick the worst possible time to be buying a house—the real estate bubble of the late '90s—and when we did finally find a couple of houses that met our criteria, we lost out on every single one in crazy bidding wars.

I finally decided that the only way we were going to get a house was if we found one before anyone else heard about it . . . and maybe even before the homeowners knew they were going to put it up for sale. Since I was fresh out of crystal balls and I do not have any psychic abilities to find something like this out, I instead came up with a plan to make up cute little flyers announcing our house needs, and stick them in the mailboxes of every house it looked like we could afford in a couple of towns where we wanted to live.

And shockingly, it worked.

A week after we stuffed mailboxes with our flyers, we got a call. The owner said he had planned on listing the house with a Realtor, but he liked my flyer and decided to let us see the house to save the Realtor fees.

The house was on a quiet cul-de-sac in the same town where we were already renting, tucked behind a split-rail fence and rows of towering pine trees, with a pretty little brook running across the front yard. Behind the house was a huge backyard with a stunning free-form pool and a swing set just begging to be used. It wasn't perfect: The kitchen and bathrooms were horribly outdated, there was wall-to-wall red carpeting with dog-pee stains throughout, and the wallpaper looked like it had been picked out by someone on a bad acid trip. But there were three bedrooms, and more important, three full baths. It was big enough, nice enough, and cheap enough that we would have some money left after we bought it to paint and pull up the red dog-pee carpeting.

"We'll take it," I exclaimed immediately after we finished the tour.

"Don't you think your husband should see it, too?" he asked.

I recalled how my husband had gotten me to agree to move to New Jersey and decided the time had come to even things up.

"He will when we move in."

. . .

In the three years we had lived in our rental house, we had accumulated enough plastic toys and kid-friendly furniture to open up our own IKEA. Although we'd only added one more kid since we'd last moved, the amount of junk we had amassed seemed to have quadrupled. Since I couldn't account for where most of it had come from, I decided there must be junk fairies that came to your house during the night and dropped off new plastic crap just to make you crazy. Sadly our kids were very attached to all our junk and when I tried to toss things, mass hysteria broke out . . . mostly from my husband when I tried to get rid of his tattered recliner with the cupholder built in and some other final remnants of his bachelor days. Ultimately I decided to let him keep the ugly recliner so I could use it for a bargaining chip later when I wanted new furniture for the new house.

When we got down to the final stretch of the move, my husband took a week off from work to help us box everything up, move to the new house, and unpack everything. But it took so long to actually pack up the old house that he had to go back to work the day after we moved into the new one. Then it was all up to me to clean the place up, unpack literally hundreds of boxes, and do all this while my kids screamed for the one toy they hadn't played with in six months that was buried in one of the hundreds of boxes. In addition to this chaos, we had to maneuver around workmen all over the house. After we'd pulled up the red carpeting with the dog-pee stains all over it, we had found that the floor underneath was also stained and needed to be refinished. Then, when we started pulling down the psychedelic wallpaper to paint, we found ten more layers of wallpaper underneath and with the final layer, the wall itself came off, so we had to have that repaired, too. Naturally we had to move into the house in the midst of all this repair work, with our hundreds of boxes, two little kids, and a mother in the throes of a nervous breakdown. It wasn't pretty.

"Do you need us to fly up and help you unpack?" my mom offered over the phone.

The idea of adding my parents to the chaos of the boxes and the toddlers and the workers did not seem like something that would help alleviate the stress for me. In fact, I was pretty sure the presence of more people in the house, no matter how well intentioned they were, would drive me over the edge and someone would end up getting boxed up with packing tape and FedEx'd back to Florida.

"I think we're doing okay," I said. "We found Emily's blankie and Josh's Pooh so I know neither of the kids are going to have an immediate meltdown. And we found a spot for Joel's reclining chair so I know he's not going to have a meltdown, either."

"How about you?" she asked.

"I found my Xanax, so I'm in good shape."

"Are you sure you don't need any help?" my mother wondered.

I looked around at the kids tearing through the boxes, the painters masking off the trim, the floor guys pulling carpet staples out of the stairs and decided I definitely needed help. But it wasn't going to come from Florida. It was probably going to come from a big bottle of Merlot . . . assuming I could find the box I had packed it in.

Chapter 11

Why You Should Pay Attention When the Sign Says, "Closed by the Board of Health"

Soon after we moved across town, I got a call from my former neighbor.

"Hi, Tracy! Would you be available to join our doubles group today?" Sharon Van DeBeek asked me over the phone. "One of the girls in our group is sick and we can't play without four."

I pulled the phone away from my ear and stared at it horrified. I realized with a start that I had just been invited to play tennis. This particular invitation was only slightly less appealing to me than being asked to go bathing suit shopping. For one thing, having seen some of the tennis ladies at Sharon's barbecue, I was fairly certain we would not have a lot in common. For another thing, and more important, I sucked at tennis. Actually, I wasn't sure if I still sucked at tennis since I hadn't played for twenty years. But I had definitely sucked at tennis when I was a teenager and I thought it was safe to assume that not playing the game for two decades had done nothing to improve my skills.

Still, I was longing to meet some other moms and I thought that if I could somehow bluff my way through the game, it might be an opportunity to make some new friends. Of course my inner voice of reason shouted at me that this was probably going to be a monumentally bad decision, but I ignored her and said yes. The whole world played tennis. All you had to do was hit a little ball with a big racket. I hit tiny little flies with newspapers all the time. How hard could this be?

After dropping my son off at school, I arrived at the tennis club early so I could rent a racket and get my daughter settled in babysitting. Then I went to the bathroom to take a final look at my outfit. Since I wasn't a tennis player, I didn't have any tennis clothes and had to make do with gym shorts, an old T-shirt, and my beat-up old sneakers. Unfortunately, my outfit did nothing to build up my confidence that this was going to be a good experience. All the other women looked like they were headed to Wimbledon. I looked like I was going to the Jersey Shore.

I arrived back at the meeting area just as Sharon and the rest of her group came in. Sharon was in the front so I couldn't see the two other women, but as they got closer, I suddenly realized I knew one of the women. It was Peanut-free Cheryl. When she saw me, her face dropped, and then she knit her eyebrows and pursed her lips.

"Hi, Tracy," said Sharon exuberantly. "This is Rena Lowenstein and this is Cheryl Hofstadter." She gestured to the two women on her right.

I smiled back a little less enthusiastically.

"Hi, Rena," I said to the lanky brunette I didn't know, and then turned to Peanut-free Cheryl.

"Cheryl and I have already met."

Cheryl attempted a smile, but it looked more like the face my daughter makes when she is trying to squeeze out a particularly large bowel movement.

All three women were dressed perfectly in pristine tennis whites with a splash of color in their skirts. I caught Cheryl checking out my outfit with a sneer. I wasn't sorry I had my gym shorts on. I was just sorry I didn't have the forethought to stuff a couple of peanut butter cups in my shorts pocket before I left the house on the off chance I would run into her so I could smush them all over her stupid smug face.

"How should we split up?" asked Sharon, seemingly oblivious to the tension between Cheryl and me.

"I'll play with Tracy!" said Rena brightly. I sighed with relief. Rena leaned over and whispered in my ear. "Sharon told me you're Jewish. Me, too," she said conspiratorially. "The Christians in this town are very cliquish. Us *Hebes* need to stick together!"

I looked at her dubiously. Although I had wanted to connect with other Jews in our community, I was not all that interested in any Jews that referred to themselves as *Hebes* and wanted my help bringing Jewish solidarity to the suburbs.

Still, I figured I was better off on the opposite side of the net from Cheryl, so I agreed.

While we waited for our court to open up, the three ladies chatted enthusiastically about Sharon and Garen's new vacation home upstate. Having seen every possible roadside attraction in the U.S., they had decided to put down some vacation roots and trade in their RV for a second home. Sharon pulled out some swatches her decorator had apparently selected for some of their furniture and the two other ladies gave their obviously experienced opinions. I did my best to look interested but decided that if I had to choose between discussing diaper wipes and cleaning products or second homes and fabric swatches, I would pick the doody conversation every time.

Fortunately our court was called and we tabled the conversation to go play. As soon as we got on the court, though, I realized that having Cheryl play across from me was the biggest mistake I made second only to agreeing to play tennis in the first place.

She served first and I was set to receive. It was clear from the onset, though, that her intention was not to get the ball past me, but rather to smash it right into me.

As the ball came soaring at me, I didn't even attempt to return the swing, but ducked my head so I didn't end up catching it in my teeth. It went past the line and hurled into the padded wall at a velocity that would have even taken out Serena Williams.

"Whoa, take it easy there, McEnroe." Sharon laughed nervously. Cheryl narrowed her eyes at her then picked up the ball again and with an icy look that would have frozen the equator, served it at me a second time.

Again the ball came at a straight trajectory toward my head. The ball grazed my ear as I dove onto the court like I was sliding into home base, narrowly avoiding being decapitated.

I glared across the net at Cheryl. I honestly didn't think our first meeting had gone so badly that she would now want to attempt to murder me with a tennis ball. True, I had unknowingly tried to bring peanut butter cups into an "alleged" peanut-free house, set up her kid to call her fat, and turned the playgroup against her, but did that really warrant my untimely demise? I wondered if maybe I was just overreacting and she was simply a very aggressive tennis player. But when she served the next ball to Rena, and it sailed gently over the net, it was clear that her aggression was all for me.

When it was my turn to receive the serve again, I panicked. I couldn't keep dodging Cheryl's serves for the rest of the game. I just wasn't that agile and besides, my husband didn't have enough insurance to cover us for child care in the case that I got beaned in the head and ended up in a coma. My only consolation, of course, was knowing that if she did hurt me, she would definitely be arrested for tennis ball battery and would probably have to go to some women's prison where she would be forced to eat peanut butter and rat dropping sandwiches every day.

As Cheryl raised her arm to serve the ball again, I suddenly shouted, "Wait." She lowered her arm and all three women looked questioningly at me.

"Did you hear that?" I asked.

"Hear what?" asked Rena.

"I thought I heard someone on the loudspeaker page me to child care. I better go see if my daughter is okay!"

I bolted off the court and ran to babysitting. I had every intention of grabbing my daughter, telling the rest of the group she was sick, and going home. I realized that they would have to end the game without me, but I didn't care. It would have been much more considerate to stick it out and certainly a lot cooler to fight back. But I thought ultimately, I'd rather be uncool and a coward than cool and dead.

. . .

Word of my tennis story spread to Lori, Becca, and Shari and the next thing I knew, I had completely won them over and they pledged their undying friendship to me. It seemed the fact that I had stood up to Peanut-free Cheryl in her home and then withstood her wrath on the tennis courts afforded me some kind of cult-hero status. I finally had the group of girl-friends I had wanted since we'd moved to the suburbs. Who cared if the basis for this friendship was a mutual nemesis. I was thrilled because they were a group of funny, bright, some-what snarky girls like me. As an added bonus, I also had no past sexual history with any of their husbands.

Maybe not so coincidentally, many of my friends were also former city girls who were having trouble adjusting to mother-hood and life in the burbs. We decided the best thing to do to settle in was desert our husbands, children, and combined sixteen loads of laundry and go for a girls' weekend getaway. Lori found a spa/resort a few hours away that promised the holy trinity of female rejuvenation: makeovers, manicures, and massages.

I was almost as excited about the spa treatments as I was about spending time with my friends. While we seemed to have a lot in common, I soon learned that they each had vastly different home lives than I did. Of all of us, I seemed to have the most stable marriage and supportive husband. It took Shari three years and five rounds of in vitro to get pregnant with her triplets, only to discover when she was seven months along that her husband had been cheating on her the whole time. Two months later she got the triplets and her husband got the boot. Lori's husband was an investment guy who came home every night wound up tighter than a Rolex, poured himself a double scotch and then locked himself in his office until dinner. He was great once he was pumped up on happy juice, but she had fears her kids would always associate the smell of scotch with their father. Becca had been a pastry chef before she got married and her husband supported her desire to go back to work after their kids were born. But after she got pregnant, he suddenly became the world's biggest chauvinist pig and decided that she should just be his little cupcake, not bake them. Although my new friends (with the exception of Shari) said they loved their husbands, and they would stand by their men, they had no qualms about abandoning them for the weekend and saying a quiet little prayer that their husbands would have to contend with no less than a double diaper explosion while they were gone.

Personally, I wasn't going away to give my husband a taste of what motherhood was like. He'd been peed on, pooped on, and done enough laundry to have earned his parental stripes. I was going to bond with my new friends and get some much-needed pampering that I was so desperately longing for. The combination of motherhood and moving had wreaked havoc on my body and mental state. I thought if I could have one completely self-indulgent weekend away from the responsibilities of motherhood and marriage, I could return to my life refreshed, renewed, and ready to find the me I had lost somewhere between giving birth and getting beaned with an assault tennis ball.

• • •

When my new girlfriends came up with the idea to go to a spa, I had visions of a luxurious place with down-covered beds, decadent food, and tons of full-body mud treatments. However, since all of us were one-income families, our budgets were decidedly less luxury resort and more BYO mud. Still, I had not taken a step without a child on my hip, in my hand, or attached to my leg for four years and I was desperate for a getaway weekend, even if I had to sleep in a tent and kill my own food.

The good news was there were no tents, just cabins. Log cabins with log beds and even log showers. Breaking up all these logs were antlers. There were antler chandeliers, antler tables, and heads with antlers covering every square inch of the lodge walls. I only hoped all those antlers came from road-kill and not some big, toothless guy named Bubba who killed Bambi's whole family with a shotgun just to decorate the lodge.

The resort was one of those faux northeast dude ranches with a twist: It was also a yoga retreat. Whoever thought to combine downward dogs with horses must have been sniffing glue when they came up with the idea. On the one hand you had a bunch of avid horsewomen who liked to walk around in chaps and smelled of hay and manure. On the other hand there were the Zen-like yoga fanatics who ate only raw foods and smelled of lavender oil. Although the yogis smelled better than the horsies, it was a toss-up whether I'd rather have an hour-long discussion about the right way to trot in a western saddle or how to open up each of my seven chakras. Since either one of these conversations would likely end the same way—with me blowing my brains out—it was fortunate that

I brought my own posse of suburban girlfriends to converse with instead.

In order to accommodate the variety of guests, the kitchen had two menus. For the horse crowd, there was a buffet each night of barbecued chicken, barbecued ribs, and what I suspected were barbecued old horses from the stables. For the yoga groupies, it was tree-bark patties and smoothies made from grass clippings. Neither of these menus really appealed to our group, so we broke the first rule of the resort and left to find some real food.

We soon noticed that while we were in the dude-ranch-slash-yoga-retreat capital of the world, there were plenty of taxidermy shops, but no restaurants or even a truck stop to speak of. After driving for thirty minutes we finally came across a combination Mexican/Chinese fast-food joint called, appropriately, Szechuan Taco. It probably should have been more aptly named Ptomaine Taco. Had we had our wits about us we might have noticed the board of health sign that had been partially removed from the front window. But we were hungry moms who had a combined nightly sleep average of about four hours, so we missed the warning and gorged ourselves on mu shu tacos and chow fun quesadillas.

Three hours later we spent the first night of our weekend getaway on the log cabin bathroom floors, heaving our Mexican/Chinese quesadillas into the log cabin toilets.

"Oh my God. Am I dead?" asked Lori the next morning at breakfast.

"I wish I was dead. Dead would feel better than this," Shari commented with her head on the table.

"Look on the bright side," I said. "I've been trying to lose the baby weight for two years. I think I dropped it all last night."

"Nice," said Shari.

"You know, I'm just starting to feel better enough to realize that I am insanely itchy. Is anyone else itchy?" I asked, scratching my legs.

"Yes, actually, now that you mention it, my arms itch like crazy," said Becca. "I wonder if we got flea bites from the horses."

"We haven't been horseback riding yet," I reminded her. "We just talked to the horsey women."

"Maybe we got flea bites from the horsey women," said Shari. We all snorted.

Lori scratched her neck furiously and then reached out to flag a passing waiter. "Can I get a Bloody Mary?" she begged.

"Oh, this is an alcohol-free resort!" said the waiter brightly. "How about a big carrot juice instead?"

Lori looked aghast—less so, I imagined, at the offer for carrot juice than the realization that we would be alcohol-free all weekend. She looked at me and I shrugged. I had no doubt we would be making another run that night to break the second rule of the resort and find a liquor store.

Becca rolled up her sleeves and peered at her arm. "Look at this. I am covered in red spots. If it's not fleas, what is it? Hives?"

I pulled up my pants legs. "Not hives. I have them too. Mosquitoes?"

"It's March," said Lori, recovering from her alcohol news shock. "There are no mosquitoes."

Shari peered intently at Becca's arm and my leg. "I thought you were all from the city," she finally remarked.

"We are," said Becca and I in unison.

"Then you should recognize those spots."

"What are they?" we wondered.

"Bedbugs."

. . .

The resort manager was reluctant to admit that they had a bedbug problem and insisted it was probably a freak early season mosquito attack. However, in an effort to maintain a happy yoga/horsey environment, he moved us to new rooms in a different wing and offered us carrot juice on the house. We gladly accepted the new rooms, passed on the carrot juice, and then snuck out in Becca's minivan to find a liquor store, anticipating we would need to get good and sloshed to fall asleep without the fear of another bedbug attack. Fortunately liquor stores were abundant in this part of the dude ranch/yoga world and we easily scored a couple of bottles of tequila.

"I want to get stinking drunk," said Shari toasting the rest of us with a shot of tequila. "I haven't had sex in four years and by the time my boys are in college and I can date again, my vagina will be so old it will shrivel up and fall off."

"Maybe by then they will have perfected the vagina transplant and you can get a snazzy new one," I suggested.

"Here's to snazzy new vaginas," slurred Lori as we all clinked glasses.

"I bet Cheryl's vagina already dried up and fell off," I sneered.

"You're confusing a vagina with a personality," said Lori.

"How did you all end up in a playgroup with her anyway?" I wondered.

"Our kids were all in the same Mom and Tot class at the library," explained Becca. "When we met her, we had no idea she was such a control freak."

"When did you realize it?" I asked.

"The first time we met at her house," she recalled. "I had some dog hair on my pants from my retriever and she got out a DustBuster and vacuumed my legs."

I burst out laughing.

"She said her kid was allergic," explained Becca.

"Just like he's allergic to peanuts?" I wondered.

"Exactly."

I shook my head. "I'm kinda sorry she's not here, though." The other women looked at me aghast.

"It would have been fun to see her with food poisoning and bedbug bites," I explained.

Everyone agreed and we passed the bottle around again to toast Cheryl, or rather, toast against her. We were sitting on the floor in the room Lori and Shari were sharing. Although we were in new rooms, none of us wanted to take the chance that we would become dinner for bedbugs again. We had already killed one bottle of tequila and were working on our second when we heard a knock on the door.

"Hey, ladies, it's time for our ten p.m. group om!" said an enthusiastic voice. We giggled like teenagers and quickly hid the bottle and shot glasses under a jacket.

"We are meditating privately," shouted Shari.

"Oh. Cool. *Namaste!*" said the voice.

"What does that mean, anyway?" asked Shari when we decided the coast was clear.

"What?" I asked.

"*Namaste.*"

"I think it means, 'We know you are in there drinking tequila, not meditating, but we are going to ignore you because you are a bunch of sad, suburban moms who are not as cool as you used to be, don't have sex, and have dried-up vaginas,'" I responded.

"Yeah," said Shari. "I thought that was what it meant."

"I have sex," said Becca. "That's how I got knocked up four times."

"That's Procreational Sex," Lori clarified. "That's not the same as Recreational Sex."

"Let's drink to Recreational Sex," said Shari. She lowered her glass. "Hey, is it still recreational if you do it alone?"

"No," I said. "Then it's Masturbational Sex."

"Oh. Too bad."

Lori refilled our glasses and we all toasted again.

"You know, I'm less bothered by the fact that I'm not having sex and more upset that I'm just not as cool as I used to be," said Lori miserably. "Do you know I couldn't find one stupid bag to bring here so I borrowed my daughter's Hello Kitty suitcase. How pathetic is that?"

"I hear ya, sista," I lamented. "At least you brought a suitcase. I had to use my son's Power Ranger backpack." I paused and had a terrible thought. "God, I hope I remember to take my vibrator out of there before I give it back to him."

My friends howled.

"My son climbed into my bed one time when I was in the shower and he found the vibrator I had left under the covers. When I came out he was holding it up and it was on," admitted Becca. "He said, 'What dis, Momma?' I was speechless. I said, 'It's a, um, back massager.' So then he took it and started rolling it over his back and saying, 'Ooh, dat feel good.' I nearly coughed up a lung."

We all laughed at this until tears came to our eyes.

As we filled up our glasses again, I noticed that my thoughts were starting to get a little fuzzy and the log room was looking infinitely cuter through the lenses of my tequila goggles.

"You know," I said thoughtfully. "Maybe if we felt better about ourselves we would feel sexier too and have more sex."

"Nah," said Becca. "I would have more sex if my kids weren't sleeping in the room next to me."

I snorted. "Okay, that, too. But I'm with Lori. I think I need to start thinking about reinventing myself. In five years I have gone from this hot, supercool working girl to a flabby full-time mom in jeans I buy from a store that also sells kitty litter."

"Yes, but it's high-end kitty litter," said Becca.

"What do you want to do, Tracy?" asked Shari, ignoring Becca.

"I don't know. But I don't want to be this person that I've become," I said gesturing to my midsection.

I really didn't have any idea what I wanted to do. I was as existentially lost as I'd ever been. When I had the kids, I assumed I would be completely fulfilled by becoming a mother, but I wasn't, and I was too ashamed to admit that to anyone, especially myself. Having a weekend away from them, I realized I missed them desperately. But I also finally had the space to realize I needed more than just housecleaning and playgroups.

"I'm not sure where I'm going with all this," I said honestly. "Maybe it's the tequila talking."

"It's talking to me!" whooped Shari. "It's saying, 'Drink more tequila!!'"

We clinked glasses again and downed another shot. I knew one thing for certain. I was going to feel like hell tomorrow.

*   *   *

After one night of food poisoning and another night of tequila pounding, none of us felt particularly rejuvenated by our spa getaway. Instead we looked like we had spent a week at Guantánamo. Other than eat and drink, we hadn't done any of the activities that the resort offered. When we planned the weekend, we'd had every intention of at least going on one trail ride. I had grown up horseback riding and I had been looking forward to getting back in the saddle, but I just didn't have the stomach for all the bouncing. Not surprisingly, none of us were into yoga, instead preferring more hostile workouts such as kickboxing and punch aerobics. Since most guests were either there for the horses or the oms, the resort didn't bother to offer much else except archery, paddleboats, and spa treatments. Considering our delicate conditions from the two nights, we all thought it would be safer to avoid shooting arrows into the air or riding around in something that could make us seasick. It was decided a good massage and mud mask would be the way to go.

I had never actually had a mud treatment and thought it might be kind of decadent to try it. The resort brochure said they used special mud flown in from Fiji that was purported to tighten your skin, smooth your cellulite, and make you look ten years younger. I wasn't sure what Fijian mud smelled like, but the mud they spackled all over my body smelled like horse manure and looked suspiciously like the mud out by the resort barn. After they covered me in the foul-smelling goo, they swathed me in something that looked like plastic kitchen wrap and left me in a room with bad new age music to let me stew in my own juices. I kept waiting for the sense of relaxation and pampering I had expected to feel, but as my body temperature rose and the smell of horse manure got more pungent, I felt nothing but the growing concern that I was turning into Mr. Ed.

"Do jew feel more relaxed?" asked the mud technician with a bizarre Russian/Spanish accent when my timer went off.

I myself could barely talk. The mud on my face had tightened so much my mouth was practically plastered shut.

"I dink so," I squeaked. I was just happy that a neigh didn't come out of my mouth.

"Goot!" she exclaimed. "Now vee vill put jew in da hot tub to loosen da mud off."

The mud technician peeled off the plastic wrap and then helped me off the table so I could waddle like a mud-covered zombie to the adjacent room with the hot tub. When I got there, I found my suburban mom posse already soaking in the tub.

"I wonder how the mud technician knew I was Jewish," I said as I eased into the hot water.

"What do you mean?" asked Lori.

"She kept asking me, 'How do *jew* feel?'" I mimicked my mud technician. "'Are *jew* relaxed?'"

"I'm not," said Lori. "This stuff smells like shit."

"Horseshit," clarified Becca.

"It's special horseshit from Fiji," I said. "It gets rid of cellulite."

"How do you know?" asked Shari.

"Have you ever seen a Fiji woman with cellulite?" I said.

"No," she responded. "But I don't think it's because they cover themselves with horseshit. I think it's because they don't steal their kids' Happy Meals."

"True that," I said.

"So . . . I got a call from Benji before we got covered in this stuff," said Becca about her husband. "He lost one of our kids."

"What do you mean, *lost*?" I wondered.

"He thought it would be fun to take them to *Chuck E. Cheese's*. When they got there the three older kids immediately climbed into the ball pit, but only two came out."

"Which one was lost?" I wondered.

"Maddie," she responded about her oldest.

"Seriously?" responded Lori. "That's horrible!"

"I know," said Becca.

"I mean it's horrible that he would let them go in the ball pit. Those things are disgusting. The balls are covered in snot and all kinds of gross kid germs."

"I agree," I added. "Letting the kids go in the ball pit is the real horror here, not losing one of your kids. You're good. You still have three."

"Thanks for your concern," said Becca wryly.

"So what happened?" asked Shari.

"I assume he hosed down the kids and put them in a decontamination chamber," I responded.

"No, what happened to Maddie?" she clarified.

"Oh. I told him to go check the bathroom," said Becca. "Ball pits make her have to go."

"Better in the bathroom than in the ball pit," I commented. "Did he find her?"

"Yes. He went into the ladies' room to look for her and

some old woman in there screamed and called security." We all laughed and then sat in compatible silence. I looked down and noticed that the water had begun to cloud up as we all demudified. I sloshed my feet around the bottom and then changed my mind and lifted them up. It felt like the squishy bottom of the lake at my old sleepaway camp that was home to numerous leeches, tadpoles, and possibly New Hampshire's answer to the Loch Ness Monster. The memory was not a particularly fond one, which probably had something to do with my lake aversion to this day.

Although the weekend had not been a rousing success so far, I realized I was finally enjoying myself as I simmered in muddy water and relished the feeling of not having to retrieve anyone's sippy cup, do laundry, or fish Barbie heads out of the toilet.

"You know what?" I said. "Aside from the bedbugs and food poisoning and hangover, this is not a bad way to spend a weekend!"

"You forgot about all those new friends we made who smell like horses and patchouli," added Lori.

"Yeah, right."

I suddenly realized that my mud was beginning to soften and break away. I rubbed some of the hot water on my exposed leg to see if my cellulite had disappeared. While I couldn't tell if I was less dimply looking than before the mud treatment, I did notice something else that was peculiar. My skin seemed to be slightly, kind of, sort of . . . green. I rubbed more water on my leg thinking it was a residue from the mud, but the green cast remained.

"Oh my God!" I yelped. "I'm green!"

• • •

"I don't know," said my dermatologist, looking over my body. "I've never seen anything like it."

"Great," I moaned. "I'm a medical anomaly." She continued to examine my exposed skin with a bright light and a high-powered magnifying glass.

"Hey, let me know if you find my old body under there," I remarked. "I think it's hiding under the cellulite."

"This is really interesting," she said ignoring me. "I think it's a stain from the mud. Or maybe a fungus."

"Fungus?!" I cried. "Like mold?"

"Probably not. I'm sure it's a stain. It should fade on its own in a couple of days. I wouldn't worry about it," she said in a slightly worried-sounding way. "Oh, and those red spots are bedbug bites."

I groaned. Our girls' weekend getaway had been a big bust. I got sick, I was a meal for bedbugs, and I turned green. If only it had rained frogs and locusts we could have called it a biblical event and made some money off it.

"Is my mommy going to stay green?" asked my son. I had both kids in the examining room with me. Mommies don't get days off for turning green.

"No, she will go back to normal soon," said the doctor.

"Good. I like her old color better."

"Me, too, sweetie," I assured him. The doctor handed me a prescription for some cream to help with the bug bites and suggested I stay away from clothes that were yellow and orange so they wouldn't clash with my skin until the green faded.

I was happy to be home, but felt a little cheated that I'd

had such a short getaway. Once I had turned green, the consensus was we should cut our losses and vacate the dude ranch. Although we thought we were probably not gone long enough for our husbands to do even one load of laundry, no one was really up for staying another night, eating barbecued horse, and sleeping with bedbugs without any alcohol to help make the situation more tolerable. Truth be told, the weekend wasn't a complete washout. If anything it gave me a renewed appreciation for everything I had at home: Good food, clean sheets, and a family that didn't smell like horseshit.

Chapter 12

It's Not Easy Being Green
(and I'm Not Talking About Recycling)

"Green isn't your color, Tray," my mother commented as she shook her head disapprovingly across the restaurant table from me. "You're better in blues and reds."

"I know, Mom. Unfortunately I wasn't given a choice as to what color my skin would turn from that mud treatment."

"I know. I'm just saying."

I sighed. I was so happy to have my mom up visiting for a few days but I was not really in the mood for a color consultation. It had been a week since the dude ranch/yoga retreat getaway and I still looked a little amphibious.

"Can we change the subject?" I asked.

"Sure."

"What's the latest gossip?" I wondered. My mother was the eyes and ears of the family rumor mill. She knew who was doing what, where, and when practically before they did. "Let me live vicariously through everyone else's lives."

"Well, let's see," she thought out loud. "Dad's cousin, Lou, has decided he is a woman trapped in a man's body and he is getting gender reassignment surgery. Your cousin, Abel, is back in rehab, and your brother, the doctor, just removed a growth from the backside of a very famous celebrity."

I gawked at her. I finally understood why I was such a basket case. My family was a freakin' three-ring circus.

"Are you serious?" I asked.

"About which part?"

"All of it."

"No. I was just kidding about your brother."

I rolled my eyes in disbelief. All this time I'd been worried that my feelings of worthlessness and self-doubt were an anomaly. It was somewhat comforting to know I probably inherited a gene for my issues, as well as the fact that surprisingly, I seemed to be the most well-adjusted member of my family, to boot.

"So, how are you doing?" she asked as she nervously looked around and then grabbed all the sugar packets and Sweet'N Low from the table and dropped them into her handbag.

"Seriously, Mom," I sighed. "Don't you have enough sugar packets at home?"

"Oh, these are cute!" she exclaimed, ignoring me as she palmed the miniaturized ketchup and mustard bottles and added them to her stash.

"*Mom!*" I hissed at her.

"Once you open these, they throw them out so I might as well take them," she explained.

"Maybe, but they're not open *yet*!"

She picked up one of the forks and examined it.

"Don't even think about it," I warned.

She scowled at me as the waiter arrived and put a basket of hot bread on the table. Her mood lifted and she dove into the bread and offered me a piece.

"I shouldn't. I still have all this baby weight to lose," I admitted sullenly.

"It's just bread, not the kitchen sink," she cajoled. I smiled. When I was little we used to celebrate our birthdays at a restaurant that served a dish called the Kitchen Sink. The bowl was the size of the table and held a staggering thirty-two scoops of ice cream, along with hot fudge, whipped cream, Reese's Pieces, and other assorted junk. My friends and I all ate from the same bowl, which was a lot of fun when we were nine but now seemed unbelievably disgusting in hindsight, not to mention, horrifically fattening.

I grabbed the bread, smeared some butter on it, and watched as it melted instantly. I popped it in my mouth and savored the sweet taste. My kids were just three and five, I rationalized to myself. I could still use the baby-weight excuse for another five years, at least.

"So, I asked how you were doing?" my mother repeated.

"I'm okay," I said through a mouthful of bread. "I started taking antidepressants." I looked at her to gauge her reaction.

"Okay," she said.

"That's it? Just, okay?"

"If that's what you need to help you feel good, then I'm glad you're doing it," she responded.

"I thought you'd be surprised," I said.

"Your one cousin is having gender reassignment surgery and another cousin is in rehab for the fourth time. No offense, but you being depressed is a blip compared to the rest of the family."

"I see your point." I nodded. "Anyway, I guess I'm doing okay. I'm trying to figure out what I want to be when I grow up."

She smiled. "I wanted to be a dancer," she said, ripping off another chunk of bread.

I gaped at her and my jaw dropped, exposing a hunk of partially chewed bread still in my mouth.

"You did? What happened?"

"You guys happened," she said. "I got out of college, married your dad, and then a year later your brother was born. And then you. And then Rich. There wasn't time anymore for dancing."

"That is so sad," I croaked. "How come you never told me this?"

"I didn't want you to feel bad for ruining my career."

I stared morosely at her. She stared back and laughed. "I'm just kidding. You guys didn't ruin my career. It was a choice. I chose motherhood!"

"Why couldn't you do both?" I wondered. Was I asking her about herself or was I really thinking about me? I wasn't sure.

"It was different back then, you know? We didn't have all the options women have today. We couldn't do it all. We did one or the other."

"But I remember you went back to work at some point," I said. "Not dancing. Teaching."

"You were seven. David was nine. Richard was in kindergarten. It seemed like the right time. And the right career choice with kids at home."

"You felt like you needed more?" I asked.

"You guys were in school full-time. What was I going to do

all day, clean the house and play bridge with my friends? That wasn't me."

I nodded. "I don't think it's me, either. Maybe I inherited that from you."

"Maybe." She smiled.

"Besides, I don't know how to play bridge," I admitted.

"Me, either." She grabbed another piece of bread, split it in half, and gave me a piece.

"But I don't want to go back to working in television and I don't know what I could do instead," I said.

"I get it," she said sympathetically. "I thought the only thing I could do was dance. And then I discovered teaching. You'll figure it out."

I smiled. "You are a wise woman, Mom."

"If I was so wise, I'd stop eating this damn bread. It's going to go straight to my behind."

"Yeah, I think I inherited that from you, too."

· · ·

Aside from my husband, my mother was the first person I'd told that I was taking antidepressants. I wasn't ashamed about it; it was just kind of a hard thing to work into a conversation. I finally decided I could use the support and began to open up to my friends about what was going on. I figured, if they judged me for being depressed, than I probably didn't want to have them for a friend, anyway. Ironically, once I started confiding in people, I was shocked to find out that just about everyone I knew was on drugs, too. Some of my friends took antidepressants, others took medicine for ADHD, and some others just sucked down Xanax like Tic Tacs to help take the edge off. With the booming business in suburban mental health pharmaceuticals, I would not have been surprised to see a sleazy guy in a trench coat hanging around outside the PTA meetings selling discounted drugs from the inside of his jacket. Since arriving in the burbs, I had been to a number of home jewelry parties, handbag parties, and bath and kitchen accessory parties. I figured it was just a matter of time before I was invited to a pill party where we could all exchange prescriptions for Prozac and Ativan. Why bother trying to score pot from the high school kid next door when you can get a few dozen Klonopin from his mom?

While a number of my friends attributed their unhappiness to postpartum depression, more, like me, found they had started sinking into an emotional abyss several years *after* their kids were born. Maybe we had experienced a chemical shift in pregnancy and childbirth that affected our moods, but if so, it was coupled with a strong feeling of being lost in suburbia. For those of us who had moved from the city, we were geographically lost, but for those of us who had defined ourselves by our careers, we felt we had lost our identities, as well. Taking antidepressants wasn't going to solve either problem. But it would certainly help me get to a place where I could address the issues without feeling like I was constantly swimming upstream. Although, ultimately, I wanted to get to a place where my identity was not based on what I did or how I looked, I still knew I wanted to get my cool back, whatever that meant, because it made me feel good about myself and set me apart from the cookie-cutter suburbanites. At that point I could figure out if I could be content simply being home with the kids, or if I wanted to go back to work in some capacity.

I was off duty three days a week, two hours a day while both kids were in school. By the time I dropped them off and then turned around to pick them up again, it was more like an hour and a half. If I hadn't showered yet that day, it got whittled down to an hour. And if I wanted the luxury of running errands without having to drag any screaming, belligerent kids in and out of the stores with me, that pretty much sucked up whatever time was left. This did not leave much time at all to even consider thinking about getting some kind of part-time job, much less actually having one. Still, something in the back of my mind was stirring. I could sense that once the kids were in school full-time, I knew I was not going to be happy being one of those moms who spent her free time playing tennis, shopping at the mall, organizing the PTA Tricky Tray fund-raiser, or volunteering for the town's Beautification Committee. I also knew I wanted to be available to my kids before and after school, and be able to stay home if they were sick or had a dentist appointment or anything like that. I had no idea what kind of job I could get that would let me work from home five hours a day and take a day off whenever I wanted unless it involved licking a bunch of envelopes or calling people on the phone to sell them burial plots. However, I was pretty sure when the time felt right, I was going to find something I was good at, that I enjoyed doing, which clearly did not involve cooking, repairing appliances, or parking my car in small spaces.

Unfortunately, it wasn't a simple answer and it probably wasn't just one thing. The good news was I was pretty sure I was on the way to discovering whatever it was that I needed to make me feel fulfilled and happy, but I realized I was going to have to do more than take a pill every day and go away to a spa once a year to figure it out. I suspected it was going to have to start on the outside and work its way in. And from that little germ of a thought, I realized I had a plan.

Chapter 13

Yes, You *Can* Be Buried in a Jewish Cemetery If You Have a Tattoo

"What's that on your ankle?" asked my husband as I dried off after my shower while he shaved at the sink. There were only the two of us in the bathroom. I felt like the grand prize winner of some kind of bathroom sweepstakes.

I grinned. "It's a tattoo."

"What is that, like one of the kids' peel-and-stick tattoos?" he wondered, bending over to examine the picture more closely.

"No, it's a real tattoo," I boasted.

"You're lying."

"Try to scratch it off," I challenged him.

He reached over and rubbed the little rosebud that was etched on the side of my leg. It didn't budge.

"Holy crap! You got a real tattoo??" he exclaimed, looking stunned. "What the heck?"

"You know I always wanted a little tattoo on my ankle," I explained. "I figured, I'm thirty-five; if I want a tattoo, I should get a tattoo."

"You know you can't get buried in a Jewish cemetery with a tattoo."

"That's not true," I argued. "My mother said the same thing when I told her I was doing this, so I asked the rabbi."

"So wait, you told your mother and the rabbi and you didn't tell me?"

"The rabbi said another member of the temple had asked him the same question," I continued, ignoring him. "So he asked a friend of his who actually runs a Jewish cemetery what the deal was. The guy said that they don't really have a problem with people who come in with tattoos. It's the guys who come in who aren't *circumcised* that are an issue."

"I would imagine."

"I guess in those instances they just do it after the fact," I suggested.

"Certainly less painful that way."

"Yeah."

He shook his head. "All that is very interesting, Tray, but I'm still a little thrown by the tattoo. Last week I came home from work and found you sitting naked in the hot tub, drinking a scotch and smoking a cigar. Now you got a tattoo. What's next? Are you going to start driving a truck?"

"Are you kidding? I can't even pull the car into the garage without hitting the wall. I don't think I could handle a truck."

"Seriously honey, what's going on? Is this like a midlife crisis or something?"

While I pondered the question my son burst into the bathroom. "Mommy, I need something for show-and-tell."

"Excuse me, can you knock?" I asked, hastily wrapping the towel around my body. Fortunately he was still at that age where naked was either hysterically funny or just something to be ignored.

"Okay," he said and turned to knock on the inside of the bathroom door.

"Not exactly what I meant."

"Ooh, can I take this?" he asked, grabbing my husband's razor.

"Oh yeah, that would go over big with the teacher," I scoffed, carefully taking the razor back.

He looked around the bathroom and his eyes fell on the image on my leg. "Heyyyy. What's that?" He sucked in a big gulp of air. "Is that a tattoooo? Is that a *real* tattoo?"

"Yes. Mom is reliving her adolescence," said my husband. I glowered at him.

"Cool. Can I take mom to school for show-and-tell?"

"Mommy, I want my sippy," announced my daughter as she entered the bathroom.

"I'm so glad we got a new house with three bathrooms so we could all end up in one bathroom again." I sighed.

"Mom got a tattoo," announced my son.

"Wassa tattoo?" asked my daughter, looking around the room for something new.

"Never mind!" exclaimed my husband and I simultaneously. "And you can't take mom in for show-and-tell, either," added my husband to my son.

"Okay, guys, everybody go downstairs and I will get *you* your sippy and help *you* find something for show-and-tell," my husband instructed. "And *you* . . ." He turned to me. "Don't add anything else until we talk about it, okay?"

"Darn, I was going to go get my tongue pierced today."

"Tracy!"

"I'm kidding." He looked dubious. "Really!"

. . .

I didn't break my promise. Cutting off all my hair wasn't adding anything. It was taking something away. I know a lot of women have their identity wrapped up in their hair. I do, too . . . but for me, it's more about *not* having hair . . . or at least having very little of it. None of this behavior should really have been any surprise to my husband. When we got married, I had long hair. Ten days after the honeymoon I cut it all off. Back then, I didn't tell him in advance that I was doing it. I just showed up at home one night with a crew cut, the same way I did with the tattoo. I don't know if I am just wildly impulsive or I'm afraid my husband will try to talk me out of doing what I want to do. Regardless of my motivation, the net result is the same: One day he went off to work and his wife had long hair and was unmarked. Then he came home at night and his wife had short hair and a tattoo. I like to think it is one of the perks of being married to me: He never quite knows what's going to happen next. I've also been known to repaint a room, retile the floors, and redecorate when my husband is out of town, without discussing it with him first. Although he usually likes the changes, this can sometimes be hazardous when he returns home late at night and walks into a couch or chair that had not been there when he left.

The first time I cut my hair off, an inebriated sailor in New York City for Fleet Week pointed to me when I walked by and yelled, "Dyke." I just pointed back and yelled, "Asshole." Typically, opinion was divided along gender lines. Women tended to like it and tell me how they wished they could wear their hair short. Men clucked their tongues and told me they would never let "their" wife wear her hair so short. I remember one time when I walked up to an ATM machine at the same time as some guy. We couldn't figure out which one of us should go first. Finally he gestured for me to go ahead.

"Ladies first," he said, chivalrously.

"Thanks!" I said brightly. "I don't hear that very much anymore."

"Maybe you'd hear it more often if you grew your hair longer," he replied.

Then there was the young boy who picked up my change purse after I dropped it on line at Dunkin' Donuts.

"Hey, mister, you dropped your wallet," he said.

I'd like to think that he was confused because he was young and I wasn't wearing any makeup that day. But when his dad told his son to give the man back his wallet, I wondered if maybe I should let my hair grow out just a little bit longer.

Gender confusion issues aside, I still was happy with the short hair. But after my son was born and we moved to the burbs, the haircut that seemed so chic in the city felt way too avant-garde for the suburbs. All of a sudden, I had this overwhelming desire to blend in, not stand out. However, as anyone who has ever tried to grow their hair out knows, timing is everything and patience is key. That said, here is a tip for anyone who is considering growing your hair out of a short cut when you are pregnant: Don't do it. It is bad enough to be the size of Texas without adding a horrible Mom Bob into the picture. Plus, the absolute least patient person in the universe is a pregnant woman. I suspect that since you know you can't do anything to make that gestational process happen any faster than the requisite nine months, you feel compelled to get immediate gratification in everything else in your life. I need to eat, *now*. I need to pee, *now*. I need a foot rub, *now*. Growing out a short haircut is the worst thing you can do for your self-esteem when you are pregnant besides sitting next to a skinny girl with perky boobs and no cellulite on the beach. It's just a bad idea.

Somehow I withstood the call of the scissors and I managed to grow my hair down to my shoulders. But once I started to come out of my early childhood coma with the help of some sleep and antidepressants, I had an epiphany that the longer locks I had painstakingly acquired were about as flattering as a double chin and would only be stylish on someone who wanted to look like the Captain and Tennille (either of them, since they both had bad hairdos).

While some women would be inclined to ease into a big hair change and go progressively shorter, I decided nothing good would be gained by going from a longish Mom Bob to a shorter Mom Bob. So two days after I got my tattoo, I dropped the kids off at their respective schools, went to the salon, and instructed the hairstylist who had held my hand through three years of growing my hair out over my ears to just cut it all off.

"Holy cow, I have cheekbones!" I announced when I saw my reflection in the mirror.

"Great haircut," commented a salon patron in the next chair.

"I wish I could wear my hair that way," said another.

I was feeling chic and gorgeous as I left the salon. Glancing at my reflection every few minutes in the rearview mirror, I drove to the preschool to pick up my daughter and grinned as she came running out to greet me. But as she got just a few feet from me, she stopped and looked around.

"Hey, Em," I called out to her. "I'm over here!"

She turned to me, her mouth dropped, and then she burst in tears.

"Mommy. Someone took your hair!" she wailed. "Make them give you your hair back!!"

Not exactly the reaction I had been hoping for.

"It's okay! I cut my hair on purpose," I assured her, kneeling down on one knee and taking her hands in mine. "That was old hair and I don't need it anymore."

She sniffled. "How come?"

"It was getting in my way," I told her, meaning both physically and metaphorically. "With my new short haircut I can spend less time doing my hair and more time playing with you!"

She frowned. "But I liked your old hair. It was soft and nice."

"My new hair is soft and nice, too," I told her. "See?" I grabbed her hand and brushed her palm across the top of my head. She giggled.

"It's spiky."

"Yup!"

"But soft."

"Uh-huh."

"What did they do with your old hair?" she asked.

"I don't know," I replied. "I think they take it and make new mommies out of it."

She giggled again.

"So what do you think?" I struck a model pose for her. She stood back with her hands on her little hips and cocked her head to the side.

"You look like a Chia Pet."

• • •

"You don't look like a Chia Pet," my husband assured me. "Your hair isn't green."

"Thanks a lot," I said, smacking him on the arm. "Seriously, what do you think?"

"I love you with long hair and I love you with short hair," he said diplomatically.

"I know you love *me*," I whined. "But what do you think of the haircut? Is it flattering?"

"Yes. It looks great. And it's very cool."

I beamed. He had said the magic word. I was cool again. Or at the very least I had a cool haircut. And a cool tattoo. That was certainly a start. I turned back to the mirror and peered at my reflection.

"You sure it doesn't make me look fat?" I asked. It was an obvious question . . . if you're a girl. Girls know that pretty much anything can make you look fat. In the female mind, even the wrong earrings can make you look fat.

He looked bewildered. "How can a haircut make you look fat?"

"It can make your face look fuller, which in turn gives the impression that the whole rest of you is too big," I explained.

He shook his head. This made about as much sense to him as looking at the back of himself in the mirror. In the male mind, if he can't see what's behind him, nobody else can, either, so why bother.

"Nobody is going to think, 'Gee, her face would look much slimmer if she had a different haircut.' They will just accept how you look with the haircut you have," he argued.

"That's true, but they might think, 'Nice haircut . . . for a cow.'"

"You don't look like a cow," he sighed. "I actually think the haircut makes your face look thinner."

"Thinner than what?"

"Than it did with your old haircut."

"Oh." I sniffed. "So you agree that a haircut *can* make you look fat."

"I guess." He sensed somehow that he was on dangerous ground and looked around to find an escape route, if it was suddenly needed.

"So you do think I'm fat?!" I demanded.

Boom.

"I'm outta here," my husband said, bolting for the door.

"I'm not fat. It's baby weight!" I yelled after him. *"Where are you going?"*

"Someplace safe," he yelled back. "A minefield or something."

• • •

Regardless of what my kids or my husband said, I knew I had made the right decision to cut off my hair and ink up my ankle. Although I was a tiny bit worried that I might be shooting myself in the foot by setting myself apart physically from the other moms in the burbs, I didn't think I had gone so far that they would run in fear from me or choose not to befriend me because I had short hair and an ankle tat. If I got a hot pink Mohawk and tattooed the words "Born to Breastfeed" across my chest, *that* might drive them away. But I thought I was probably safe with a pixie cut and a little rose tattoo on my leg. It was just enough to make me feel unique and somewhat cool again without being so over the top that the suburbanites would come to my home with torches blazing and try to run me out of town.

Fortunately, my new friends loved my haircut and tattoo, as I knew they would, and within a few weeks, they had all gotten inked, too. Lori got a tattoo ankle bracelet, which immediately inspired her daughter to draw one around her baby sister's ankle with a permanent marker. Becca got a cute little cupcake on her hip to motivate her to reclaim her bakery dream one day. And Shari got a pair of angel wings on her back because she said it was divine intervention that she didn't cut off her husband's balls when she found out he had cheated on her after five rounds of in vitro. I was flattered that they all decided to follow me and do something to literally mark their roads back to individuality, but I was also glad no one chose to cut their hair off like I had. I wanted something that was dramatic, different, and all mine.

Chapter 14

Where I Join a Gym and Flatten My Kickboxing Partner

Cutting my hair and getting a tattoo were great first steps to coolness because they were quick and easy. Losing the baby weight I had put on from two pregnancies and a truckload of Krispy Kreme doughnuts was going to take a little longer. All the experts advocate a sensible eating plan and exercise, but trying to accomplish either of those with two little kids and a mountain of junk food around was definitely a challenge.

Since I figured it would be easier to work out an hour a day than keep my mouth shut for twelve hours, I decided to tackle the issue of exercise first. However, with one kid only in school for half the day and the other only in three times a week for about two hours a day, it was tough to find the time to get to the gym and still be able to jam in all those bazillion other things I had to do during my "free" time. Taking them to child care at the gym was not an option. The one time I took them was the day my son pushed my daughter into a wall and she ended up in the hospital getting a forehead full of stitches. This did not really endear us to the child care people and they hinted that I might not want to bring the kids back there again until they were a little older, like, say, thirty.

Truth be told, I was not a big exercise person as it was, so it did not take much to dissuade me from joining a gym. Besides the fact that I did not like to sweat, I was really intimidated by all the hard-core health club–aholics. Looking at all the other women running mini-marathons on the treadmills, bench-pressing their body weight in barbells, and flexing their Madonna-like muscles in the mirror-covered walls always made me want to run screaming to the nearest Carvel in defeat.

The other problem was, I figured if I was noticing them, all those people could hardly miss me gasping for breath after five minutes on the StairMaster. And that was just to program the darn thing.

Once I got pregnant, I thought I had gotten a free pass to skip the gym. Unfortunately, the ob-gyn told me it would be good for me *and* the baby to keep exercising. I told her that (a) one has to *be* exercising in order to *keep* exercising, and (b) it is awfully hard to exercise when you are puking all the time. Had I actually been able to exercise during pregnancy, I might have only put on fifty pounds of doughnut weight, rather than the sixty. But that is all cellulite under the bridge.

Since summer was approaching and the thought of me in a bathing suit was much more frightening than the thought of having people laugh at me falling off a treadmill, I finally decided to suck it up and commit to a workout regimen. Having been banned from my previous gym, I decided to join another gym in town where they had never heard of me and my devil children. Unfortunately, the only other gym was the club where I had gone to play tennis with my neighbor Sharon Van DeBeek, the leader of the Suburban Jewish Ladies Coalition, Rena, and my archenemy Peanut-free Cheryl. Most people either had a tennis membership or a gym membership, though, and there were separate entrances for the two clubs, so I figured it was unlikely I would run into any of them when I went to work out.

Armed with an iPod and a photo of a fat lady in a bikini, I sweated, I huffed, I puffed, and then eventually I got to the top of the stairs of the gym entrance to work out. I guess I should not have been surprised that I was so winded. I had not done anything that resembled exercise since I ran into the emergency room with my legs crossed so my daughter wouldn't slide out and be born in the hospital parking lot. Still, I didn't realize how sadly out of shape I had become until I started hyperventilating about five minutes into my preprogrammed thirty-minute run on the elliptical.

Deciding no one could be that pathetically out of shape, I figured it must not be me, it must be the machine. I carefully dismounted the elliptical and went to find a trainer.

"Is this set wrong?" I asked the trainer on duty, gesturing to the dashboard of the elliptical.

"What do you mean?" he responded. His neck was about as thick as my thighs and he spoke with an accent that made me think he was trying to sound like Arnold Schwarzenegger.

"Did someone make the default setting the highest setting?" I asked.

He looked confused and peered down at the digital display.

"No. Actually, the default setting is the lowest setting," he proclaimed.

"Well, I think the calibration is off," I responded assuredly. "It feels like it's set for 'ten,' not 'one.'"

He jumped on the elliptical and started jogging easily.

"Nope. Feels like a 'one' to me," he said.

"Yeah, well you do Ironman Triathlons during your lunch hour," I quipped. "I think the machine is off." He shrugged and walked away. I jumped onto another machine, made sure it was set to 'one,' and started jogging. Within five minutes I was convinced I was climbing Mount Kilimanjaro.

"I think *all* these ellipticals are screwed up," I announced to no one in particular.

Since this seemed like an obvious time to take a break, I ran down to child care to check on my daughter and make sure she hadn't taken any Barbie dolls hostage. Then I headed back to the gym floor to resume my workout. But as I rounded the corner, I ran into another mom from my son's school.

"Hey, I didn't know you belonged here!" she exclaimed.

"Actually, I just joined today."

"Great! What do you think so far?" she asked.

"It seems good. None of the ellipticals work though."

"Really?" she responded quizzically. "That's weird." I nodded vigorously. As I stood there in my ratty gym shorts and frayed tank top, I noticed that she was dressed in a perfect exercise ensemble. One of the reasons I had joined the gym was because I'd heard that a lot of other moms from my area belonged there and I was hoping to connect with them and find some workout buddies. However, I knew this particular woman worked out just about every day, actually jogged to the gym before her workout, and played multiple sets of tennis after she was done. She was in better shape than I had ever been and probably ever would be and looked like she could bench-press me and the car I drove (not jogged) to the gym in. That being the case, there was not a chance in hell I would choose her for a workout buddy and thought I might, actually, even bring her a gift box of Krispy Kremes one day just to mess with her obvious plan to rule the world.

"Hey, what are you doing right now?" she asked.

"Um, working out," I said. Duh.

"There is a kickboxing class starting in a few minutes," she told me. "You should come try it!" I hadn't thought about jumping into any classes right away, but since it worked with my schedule, I thought it might be worth doing. In addition to being fun, it seemed like an exercise that was actually useful: I could lose weight, get in shape, and learn some great boxing techniques to use on the next person who asked me when my nonexistent baby was due.

As I entered the room, I noticed that the kickboxing instructor was so buff she looked like Linda Hamilton in the second *Terminator* movie and, therefore, I assumed, was probably messing around with Arnold Schwarzenegger upstairs. However, I was relieved to see that most of the other members taking the class were flabby, post-baby body-challenged women like me. But as I scanned the room, my eyes suddenly fell on the one person I had hoped never to run into again. Peanut-free Cheryl glared at me from her spot across the room, and I said a silent prayer thanking God that there were no tennis balls anywhere in the room.

Although most of the other women looked like they were

out of shape like me, once the class started, I soon realized that these women meant business, specifically one in particular, and if I pissed anyone off, I was gonna get my post-baby butt kicked. As we started to bob and weave, the instructor suggested we picture someone's face on the mirror that we didn't like. From the way the other moms were doing their roundhouse kicks and punches, I was pretty sure they were visualizing either their husbands or their mothers-in-law, or perhaps another mom. Either way, it was clear from the get-go that this was a pretty angry group and I was going to fit right in.

I was doing a fairly good job of keeping up until we started a sequence of jab-cross-hook-upper-cuts mixed with these step-to-side kicks. I didn't recall ever seeing George Foreman do this move when he was a boxer, and if he did, it would probably explain why he left the boxing world to make grills instead.

All of the other moms seemed to have no problem with this combination. But for me, the girl who got thrown out of second-grade ballet class for tripping over my own feet and knocking over all the other dancing daisies and making them cry, this was beyond my capabilities. Although I was very good at picturing the face of someone who really got my goat, I just could not coordinate the whole punch-step-kick-punch thing without looking like a palsied Rockette.

"Jab-cross-hook-upper-cut," yelled the instructor at me from the front of the room.

"I'm doing that," I argued.

"No. Cross. *Cross!*" she yelled at me, demonstrating a move that looked vastly different from the one I was doing.

"I'm crossing!!" I yelled back, breathlessly. I had barely

enough air to jab and kick at the same time much less respond
to the instructor.

"That's not right. Those are two jabs," she said, clearly exas-
perated with me. I'm not sure why she expected someone
whose job duties included washing dishes, doing laundry, and
making chicken nuggets to instinctively know how to be a
martial arts expert. The only person I'd ever punched in my
life was a New York City mugger who tried to steal my laundry
bag on the subway. And even then, I didn't really punch him
so much as beat him with my bag.

While I was simultaneously trying to kickbox and blend in
with the wall, the instructor looked around and then pointed
at Peanut-free Cheryl.

"Cheryl," she barked. "Go show our newcomer how to do
a cross."

Cheryl reluctantly left her spot across the room and walked
over to me.

"This is a jab," she said demonstrating a jab. "And this is a
cross," she said throwing a cross punch into the air while I
kept flailing my arms around like a drowning swimmer.

I watched her and then started jabbing again.

Exhaling loudly in frustration, she leaned in and grabbed
one of my jabbing arms to show me the cross, and as she did,
I crossed with my other fist, connected with her jaw, and
knocked her flat off her feet.

The whole class stopped punching and kicking and just
stared. I was simultaneously appalled and delighted. I tried to
suppress my smile.

The instructor stopped jabbing and grinned at me across
the room.

"*That* was a cross."

. . .

After knocking Cheryl out by accident, I realized I *had* to keep going back to the gym so I could get in shape for the day that she would hunt me down and try to kill me. I assumed she was a pacifist since she didn't let her kid play with any toy guns, and figured when she came for me, it wouldn't be with an Uzi or a machete, but rather she'd bring her formidable weight to bear and would try to crush me with a full body slam. I thought my only chance at survival was to build muscle mass so I could withstand the force of her well-endowed suburban ass on my chest. It was either that or improve my endurance and try to outrun her.

Either way, the threat of Death by Cheryl was a great motivator to keep me going back to the gym. I avoided the kickboxing class because I was fairly certain lightning would not strike twice in the same workout room, and instead tried spinning. This seemed like the perfect workout for me. Safely strapped into my own stationary bike, I could neither tip over nor ride into oncoming traffic, nor could I physically interact with the other riders and accidentally cause personal injury to someone else. The room was dark, the music blared, and the instructor yelled at us to "get our candy asses up the goddamn hill." As I sweated and huffed my way through an imaginary Tour de France, I realized I had finally found my exercise nirvana. If we could wrap it all up with mojitos at the end of the ride, my life would have been complete.

The best part, though, was that the same people came back to the same spin class I went to every week. In the beginning I stayed silent while they bantered about things they had discussed at previous spins and I had no idea what they were talking about. But after a while I found I could share in the conversations and I was accepted into the Spin Circle as one of them. I would not consider myself a jock by any means, and I was pretty sure that if I participated in an actual bike race, outside, on real streets, I wouldn't make it past the first Dunkin' Donuts without dismounting and gorging myself on a dozen munchkins. But inside the spin room, I was just as much of a virtual athlete as the rest of them and I was happy to be considered part of the group.

It was about my third month into my workouts that I suddenly noticed my thighs had gotten a little firmer, my butt a little tighter, and my baby belly just a tiny bit less jiggly. I still couldn't fit into my pre-baby clothes comfortably and I was fairly certain I couldn't take Cheryl if she came at me, but it was the first time in more than five years that I could see a glimmer of the body I used to have and the cool chick I used to be.

Chapter 15

Sometimes Eating Like a Grown-Up Means Giving Up the Cheez Doodles

Most nutritionists stress fruits, vegetables, and lean protein as the main elements of a healthy weight-loss plan, with just a small amount of carbohydrates thrown in to keep you from blowing your diet on a premenstrual Ring Ding binge. This, unfortunately, was the exact opposite of what my kids would eat. They favored foods that were white—potatoes, pasta, pizza—and they had a preference for food-esque items that came in paper bags with crappy toys inside. Much as I'd like to blame this on media influences, the fault for their fast-food addiction was all mine. When I was pregnant with my daughter, I would get obscene fast-food cravings. I tried not to indulge in those urges too often, but apparently I must have frequented more than a few drive-throughs during those nine months. I realized this the day my husband and I were driving with my son in the car and as we passed a McDonald's, my son looked out the window, saw the giant "M," and yelled, *"Fen fies!!"*

"How does he know you get french fries at McDonald's?" my husband asked me suspiciously. It was a fair question considering we had an agreement that we would not give our kids fast food.

"He must have seen it on TV," I punted.

"I thought he just watched the public station with no advertising," he said. It was a fair assumption considering we had an agreement that our kids would only watch shows on PBS.

"I think Elmo eats McDonald's french fries on *Sesame Street*," I responded.

"Nice try there, french fry girl, but you're so busted."

"Yeah, whatever. At least he didn't tell you about the breakfasts at Burger King."

Although I had started working out, I suspected that the antidepressants were sabotaging my weight-loss efforts. I didn't know by exactly how much because I had smashed my scale to smithereens the last time I was pregnant and saw the arrow start swinging ominously toward the 175-pound mark. However, when I noticed that I was the only one in the family whose jeans seemed to be significantly shrinking in the dryer, I deduced that I might have put on some extra weight. Unfortunately, I had not had the opportunity to smash my doctor's scale to smithereens, and when I went for my annual physical, the shlit hit the flan. I recounted the traumatic event for my husband:

Me: I had a physical yesterday.
Husband: How did that go?

Me: It was *horrible*!! The doctor said I'm fat!! *Huge!* Like Shamu the whale, but bigger! He said I have to go on a major diet right away! We're eating nothing but grapefruit for the rest of our lives and if that doesn't work I'm getting full-body lipo!!!!

Husband: How much weight did you gain, really?

Me: Five pounds.

My husband really could not understand what all the drama was about. He shrugged, said some of it was probably muscle mass from spinning, and left to go find a power tool to terrorize. I realized at that moment that the issue of weight gain is definitely one of those male/female things. If a woman is told by her doctor that she's put on some weight since her last visit, after gouging his eyes out and destroying his scale, she will cry for days and spiral into a dark depression that only chocolate could save her from. But a man? He shrugs, buys pants one size bigger in the waist, and goes back to his Ben & Jerry's without incident.

Unfortunately for the men, they don't realize how much they're missing by not having weight issues. Without the experience of overreacting to the news that they've gained weight, they can never respond with the joy of "the denial."

Typically, after I have finished my crying jag, I will inform my doctor and anyone else who will listen that any weight they say I've gained is not true fat but either pre-, during-, or post-menstrual bloat. I will also mention that my scale at the gym is five pounds lighter than the one in the doctor's office, which *clearly* needs to be calibrated, *and* my appointment was in the afternoon when everyone knows you weigh much more than your *true* morning weight. If anyone is still listening to me at this point and certainly must either be in a coma or dead to still be paying attention, I will further tell them that I also ate a lot of fiber the day before and will weigh significantly less after my next trip to the bathroom.

Pregnancy cravings aside, I have to admit, I have never been the healthiest eater. When I was growing up, my mother was a leader in the war against junk food. Way before organic and farm-raised foods were in fashion, she banned white bread and bologna from the premises. There was nary a Cheeto, Dorito, or Frito in our house. While I always assumed my mother had our best interests at heart, it turned out the reason that she did this was so *she* wouldn't be tempted by the stuff. Years later I found her stash of frozen candy bars hidden in the freezer and then the Kit Kat was out of the bag.

One would assume that with this kind of upbringing, I would develop a lifelong appreciation for healthy foods. But I knew what I was missing. I saw the way the other half lived and I wanted to be part of the Hostess family, too. So while some kids picked their friends based on similar interests or great Barbie collections, I would make playdates based on who had what in their pantries. When my mother gave me an apple for a snack in my lunch bag, I would skip off to school and trade it to some kid for his Little Debbies. I was leading a double food life: I grew up on granola and yogurt in the home: Twinkies and Oreos outside of it. Thinking that maybe my kids should have a better balance on the whole junk-food-versus-healthy-food issue, I kept some junky food in the house and tried to set limits on how much they could eat and when. The junky food was kept, of course, in "the Junky Cabinet." Over time the Junky Cabinet became two Junky Cabinets as my kids wore down my healthy resolve and talked me into buying the latest cheesy this and the newest chocolatey that. Soon word got out in the neighborhood that we had more junk food than the floor of a movie theater cineplex. When I came home one day and found six kids I didn't know foraging through the Junky Cabinet, I suspected the healthy/junky balance might have swung a little too far in the wrong direction.

While my kids managed to figure out how much good stuff to eat versus how much sugary stuff, I never did. Not surprisingly the worst time for me was between Halloween and Valentine's Day when it seemed we always had enough candy on hand to put a diabetic elephant into shock. Since that accounted for roughly half the year, it didn't take a math genius to figure out how much cellulite a nearly middle-aged mother of two could amass eating candy every day for five or six months. Factor in all the leftover mac and cheese my kids didn't eat, the extra chicken nuggets, and the uneaten peanut butter and jelly sandwiches, and it was just a matter of time before I actually started to *resemble* a diabetic elephant.

Having been down this diet road a couple hundred times before, I was familiar with just about every weight-loss gimmick out there. Although my sensible husband suggested I make changes that I could stick with for life, I instead preferred to try one of the Hollywood diets that the celebs do after they have a baby so they can drop the baby weight a week after giving birth. While it occurred to me that living on a concoction of maple syrup and lemon juice for two weeks might not be the healthiest way to lose a few pounds, I was pretty much willing to do anything that would allow me to get thin quick in the hope that I would lose *too* much weight and be able to eat my way back up. Unfortunately this diet worked about as well for me as the condom my husband wore when I got pregnant. I would only be on the diet for a day or two before I got massive cravings from the smell of the maple syrup and gorged myself on pancakes and waffles.

After failing the maple syrup diet, I decided to give one of the high-protein diets a try. A lot of my friends had done these and the weight seemed to melt right off. Having existed on large quantities of sloppy joes and cheeseburgers when I was pregnant and in the throes of massive meat cravings, I thought this might be the perfect diet for me. I did actually manage to lose six pounds the first month and was prepared to ride the bacon wave all the way to the skinny beach until I checked back in with my doctor and found out that my cholesterol had skyrocketed one hundred points in four weeks.

"You need to do a different diet," he told me over the phone when the results came back.

"But this one is working for me," I protested. "I just bought new skinny jeans!"

"That's great," he responded. "But no one will see you in them if you have a stroke."

"I could wear them in rehab," I murmured.

"Go do Weight Watchers," he suggested.

"Ugh. I hate that," I said. "It's like AA for fat people. Everyone sits around and talks about their dysfunctional food relationships. Then they all join hands, sing 'Kumbaya,' and count how many points they have left to eat that day. No, thanks. I'd rather have a stroke."

"I think you need some support."

"That's why I wear Spanx," I commented.

"No, I mean people support. Like a group or a friend."

Although his plan was good in theory, I was pretty sure I

wouldn't be welcomed to any group. The one time I did do a group diet class and they asked us to picture ourselves thin, I nearly started a riot when I said that the only thing I could picture right then was digging into a warm chocolate lava cake.

"I don't really need the support. What I need is someone just to tell me what to eat so I don't have to think about it," I said to my doctor. "Left to my own devices, I will eat a pepperoni pizza and justify it by saying it was a healthy choice because it featured the four major food groups."

"It is a good choice . . . if you eat one slice," he responded. "Not if you eat the whole pie."

Having been my physician since we got to the burbs, my doctor knew my MO. He had seen me at my thinnest and my heaviest, from mom jeans to skinny jeans and back again. He didn't care if I looked cool or frumpy, as long as I was healthy. And twenty-five pounds overweight with a cholesterol level of 315 was definitely not healthy.

"Okay, fine," I conceded. "I'll call Jenny Craig."

"Good. Give her my regards."

. . .

When you go to a dentist's office, you generally have the expectation that all the employees will have gleaming white teeth. Similarly, when you go to a diet place, you expect all the workers there will be thin. This being the case, I was a little unnerved when I arrived at the local Jenny Craig and saw that, of everyone there, I was actually the thinnest. I wondered if maybe they thought that clients would feel threatened if all the employees were stick thin. Or maybe they wanted the clients to feel solidarity with the employees who were also struggling with their own weight issues. However, if the two-hundred-pound woman behind the counter represented a Jenny success story, I seriously hoped she had started out significantly larger than she was now.

The Jenny advisor who was assigned to me seemed to represent a Jenny client both before and after. From the waist up, she was tiny. From the hips down, she looked like she had swallowed an open umbrella.

"I've been on Jenny for a year and I'm doing the maintenance part of the plan now," she told me enthusiastically as she tried to wedge her bottom half into the narrow desk chair.

"Really?" I wondered. "So you reached your goal?"

"Oh yes," she boasted. "And then some!"

I decided her goal must have just been from the waist up.

"Of course I still have some junk in my trunk," she said, laughing as she slapped her butt with her hand. "But my boyfriend says he likes to have something to hold on to!"

I grinned with relief. I had been worried that there was something about the program that made you lose weight in only half your body. But apparently Joellen stopped dieting by choice while she still had her bodacious behind. I was relieved that going on Jenny Craig would not have me end up with skinny arms and fat nostrils.

"So let's talk about you!" she said. "Why are you here?"

"My doctor said I am too thin and I need to gain weight."

She looked at me curiously.

"Sorry. Wishful thinking," I said. "I need to lose twenty-five pounds and I'd like to do it without thinking too much, suffering too much, or giving up french fries."

"Well, I can help you with the thinking and suffering parts. But you may have to take a break from the french fries for a while."

"I kind of figured," I admitted. "And I don't suppose Krispy Kremes are on the menu, either?"

"No, but we have really delicious chocolate, peanut butter *Anytime bars*," she said, whipping one out from her desk drawer. It was three inches long, a quarter-inch thick, and looked about as appetizing as a cardboard bookmark.

"So anytime I want a Krispy Kreme I should have an Anytime bar?" I wondered.

"No. You can have your Anytime bar anytime you want it, but only once a day."

"Then they should call it a Onetime bar."

She thought for a minute. "But then you wouldn't know you could have it anytime."

"I can't have it anytime," I said. "I can only have it one time."

"But that one time can be anytime!" she declared.

"It's misleading," I told her. "They should call it the 'Anytime You Want It But Only One Time a Day' bar."

"I think that would be too long to fit on the wrapper," she said.

"Well, then maybe they should make the damn bars bigger," I yelled.

She looked at the bar as though she were considering my suggestion.

"If they were bigger, they'd have more calories and then you couldn't have them anytime," she said patiently.

"You can't have them anytime anyway," I pouted. "You can only have them one time, remember."

"Yes, but that one time can be anytime," she repeated.

I sighed. No matter what time I had it, it was still going to taste like a bookmark, so I gave up and suggested we move on.

"Okay, let's go weigh you in!" Joellen announced.

"Hang on," I responded. "I think I need some more clari-fication on those Anytime bars!!"

. . .

After I got weighed, measured, and consoled, I picked out an appetizing array of meals for the next week. I liked the fact that I didn't have to think about what I could make to stay on my diet, and with options like mac and cheese, I could eat exactly what the kids were eating. I wasn't sure how I was going to make it work if we went out to eat, but I figured I would cross that food bridge when I got to it. Worst-case scenario, I could order a salad, bring my Anytime bar, and chew on the restau-rant napkins if I was still hungry.

Not surprisingly with all this talk about food, by the time I got home from my Jenny consultation, I was famished. I dumped all my packages on the table and tore into one of the lunches. The picture on the box looked great, but as I peeled off the cellophane covering the dish, I had to squint to find the food. The portion was tiny. It was about a third of the size of what I would usually eat for a meal. It was so small it looked like a meal for our pet hamster. Actually the hamster himself would have been a bigger meal than the Jenny meal. Not that I would eat our pet hamster. Unless, of course, I was starving and there were french fries on the side.

Somehow I managed to get through the first week of my Jenny diet without eating the entire box of Anytime bars in one sitting or eating the box itself, which would have essentially tasted the same as the bars but with fewer calories. While I was consumed by the Hunger That Ate the Universe for the first few days, I soon realized that all the fiber they packed into the food was indeed filling me up. Unfortunately, that fiber had to go somewhere and for me, it seemed my body's natural inclination was to turn it into gas.

"Um, honey," said my husband one night, wrinkling up his nose. "Are you having some digestive issues?"

"Maybe," I admitted reluctantly. "I think it's this diet I'm on. The prepackaged food is gassing me up!"

"Well, could you figure it out?" he asked covering his face with a sofa pillow. "Soon!"

"I'll look into it," I promised as I let another one fly. My son jumped up and ran out of the room.

"Coward!" I yelled after him.

I turned to my husband. "You know, I've been thinking that we should get a dog."

"A dog? That's random. Why do you want a dog?" he asked from under his pillow.

"So I have someone to blame the gas on."

Chapter 16

Pet Smart and a Pound Foolish

"You were just kidding about the dog, right?" my husband asked a few days later as we got ready for bed.

"What dog?" I wondered.

"You said you wanted to get a dog to blame your gas on."

"Ha!" I laughed. "Yeah, I was kidding. I'm so hungry on this stupid diet that if we got a dog, I'd probably eat him." I walked into my closet to get my pajamas and stood thinking for a minute.

"Okay, good," shouted my husband across the room to me. "I mean the part about not getting a dog, not the part about eating it."

"Although," I mused, poking my head back out. "Maybe it might be a good time to get a dog. The kids have been asking and we do have room in the house and a decent dog backyard . . ."

My husband shook his head vehemently. "It's *not* a good time. It's actually a really bad time," he assured me.

"Why do you say that?" I asked, suddenly warming to the idea. I came back out and sat down on the bed. "Dogs teach kids responsibility and unconditional love and the dog can watch the kids when I have to go pick up the dry cleaning."

"The dog won't be Nana from *Peter Pan*, honey," he said. "And seriously, let's be real, the kids are four and six. The only one who is going to be responsible for taking care of the dog is you. How are you going to like cleaning up after a dog when doody diapers make you gag?"

He had a point, but I wasn't ready to give up just yet. As I prepared my next argument, we heard a knock on the door. Both kids stood in the doorway in their pajamas.

"Hey, you guys are supposed to be in bed," my husband said.

"We heard you talking about a dog," said my son. My daughter nodded her head vigorously.

"Are we getting a dog?" he asked hopefully.

"We're not getting a dog. Not right now," said my husband, glaring at me.

Both kids and I pouted.

Josh thought for a minute. "Well, how about a tarantula. Could we get a tarantula?"

I gasped. "*No. No* tarantula!"

"How about a scorpion? Or an anaconda?"

"No," I exclaimed. "I draw the line at pets that can poison or swallow you."

"I want a kitten and I want to name it 'Pussy,'" my daughter said softly. My husband and I looked at each other and burst out laughing.

"What?" she wondered.

"We have two kids and one sometimes eats off the floor," my husband said, looking at my daughter. "We don't need a pet."

"What about a llama?" I suggested playfully. "We can get an alpaca and I can shear it and knit us all sweaters."

The kids jumped up and down. "Yeah!" cheered my son. "Llamas are cool. They spit."

"I want a kitten called 'Pussy,'" Emily repeated.

"We got it, Em," said my husband, picking her up and sitting her on his knee. He turned to me. "Yeah, honey, you're gonna shear a llama and knit us sweaters? You can't even sew a button without drawing blood."

I made a face at him.

"The Plopkins next door got a frog," said Josh.

"Plotkin. With a 'T,'" responded my husband. "No, they have a son who thinks he's a frog. That's different."

I could see the wheels turning in my son's head.

"Hey, if we got a llama, I could ride it to school and then you wouldn't have to drive me," he offered.

"Really?" I said. "What are you going to do with the llama when you go into school?"

"Tie it to the bike rack."

"You can't take it to school because it might spit on the principal and then you'll get in trouble," said my daughter, the voice of reason. "Someone in my class brought her little brother into school and he spit on the principal and she got into trouble."

"How about a pig?" I suggested. "You know, like a potbellied pig? They're very smart. You can housebreak them."

"Potbellied pigs can get to be two hundred pounds," commented my husband. He shook his head. "I can't even believe we're having this conversation, anyway."

"Do pigs spit?" wondered my daughter.

"Pigs happen to be very clean and they eat garbage so it can help us cut down on the amount of trash we generate," I assured them.

"How about a goat," Josh wondered. "They eat garbage, too, plus we can milk a goat!"

"Ewww. I don't want to drink milk from a goat," Emily moaned.

"You drink milk from a cow," said her brother.

"I do? Ewwww. Does chocolate milk come from a cow, too?"

"Yeah, a chocolate cow."

"Josh, don't mess with your sister," I reprimanded him. "Em, they add the chocolate later."

"Yeah, chocolate comes from llamas," my son added.

"Oooh, I wanna llama!" my daughter cried, clapping her hands. "And we can name it 'Pussy.'"

My husband had had enough. He got up and deposited our daughter back in the doorway. "No goats or pigs or llamas or tarantulas or scorpions or anacondas!"

"How about a pygmy pig?" I said softly.

"No pigs!!"

"Okay then," I said. "How about a dog?"

My husband nodded. "At least a dog is an actual pet."

"Great, I'll look for one! Come on you guys," I said ushering the kids out of the room. "It's late. Get back to bed. We'll talk more about llamas and pigs tomorrow, okay?"

I guided both kids back to their rooms, kissed them good night, and went back to my bedroom. My husband stood in the middle of the room with his hands on his hips.

"All that llama and pig business was just a bait and switch to get me to agree to a dog, wasn't it?"

"I have no idea what you're talking about," I said innocently. "I just thought a dog really would be good for the kids. And it would be nice for me to have the company when the kids are at school during the day!"

He looked at me in disbelief. "Do you hear yourself? You have been complaining for years that you don't have any time for yourself and now that you finally have a couple of hours alone each day, you want to stuff a dog into it? That's insane."

I stormed off to the bathroom. While I washed my face and brushed my teeth, I tried to wonder why, all of a sudden, I had this burning desire for a dog. My husband had pointed out recently that it seemed like life was just starting to get a little easier. Why, at the first sign of relief, was I looking to muck everything up again? I guess the good news was I wasn't considering another baby. But why a dog? Why now?

I wondered if a dog was a simple solution to what I was really craving. I knew I was missing something in my life and I couldn't figure out what that something was. Rather than sit with it, let it percolate and reveal itself, I wanted to rush in and fill the hole with something so I didn't have to continue to live with the discomfort of not knowing. Much as I hated to admit it, my husband was right: getting a puppy wouldn't make things better. It would be a huge distraction from my process of discovering what I really needed in my life. Yes, it would be a cute and loveable distraction, but a distraction nonetheless. Dogs are messy and needy, just like kids. They get sick and need doctor appointments and they need to be fed and cleaned and given lots of attention, just like kids. I didn't need another kid and I didn't need a dog. I needed an answer.

. . .

I really had thought things would get less complicated as my kids got older and they were able to do more and more things for themselves. But I soon learned that life has a way of getting more complex as your kids get older, not less. There are school schedules and after-school schedules and all kinds of logistical issues to figure out that are not an issue when your kids are infants and you can strap them to your chest and do whatever you please, as long as you can take a break for the occasional feeding or exploding diaper.

The other noticeable difference is that babies don't argue with you and usually stay where you put them, eat what you tell them, and go where you take them. But from the moment your kid turns two and discovers the word "no," the stage is set for all future battles, from what they are going to wear (or not wear) to who they are going to hang out with. Child psychologists call this "Individualization," and it's an important developmental milestone for kids so they can begin to separate from you, the parents, and develop their own sense of self. Personally, I think this step is highly overrated and I would be much happier if the kids just continued to do whatever the heck I told them to do.

Life with kids isn't the only thing that gets more complicated. Relationships also change, as do the people who are in them, and it wasn't long before I started to see marriages that had been rock solid before kids begin to erode after kids, and by the time elementary school rolled around, divorce papers were being served. The first of my friends to split from their husbands, of course, had been Shari, although that happened both before we became friends and before her kids were born.

Although the other girls bitched about their husbands, I thought they, like me, would stick it out and try to ride out the bumps in the marital road. However, for my friend Lori, the bumps became gaping sinkholes, and soon after returning from our girls' weekend getaway disaster, she decided she'd had enough of her husband's schmucky behavior and she took action. One night he came home and went to the liquor cabinet to pour himself a drink, like he always did, without so much as saying hi to his wife or kids, like he never did, and when he got there, he found all the booze was gone, and, coincidentally, so were Lori and the kids.

"Where are you staying?" I asked her when the four of us got together for our bimonthly, moms-only, ladies-who-lunch-but-don't-wear-pink-and-green outing. We had initiated this ritual when the kids' schedules became so insane that it had become almost impossible to get together for regular playdates anymore. There was, admittedly, less lunching and more drinking at our lunches, but since we started early and finished at least three hours before school pickup, most of us were mostly sober by the time we had to get the kids.

"At my mother-in-law's, believe it or not," said Lori. "She always liked me better than him."

"Why?" asked Becca. "'Cuz you're a better daughter-in-law than he is a son?"

"No, because I'm not a lying sack of shit who cares more about his booze and his money than his kids."

"That makes sense," I responded and then squinted my eyes at her. She talked a good game, but I knew Lori was pretty distraught about the situation. She had picket-fence dreams and ended up with a pothole marriage. As sucky as I had felt over the past five years, I knew the kids and I were my husband's first priority. Assuming, of course, we had at least one working bathroom.

"Are you okay?" I asked.

"So-so," she answered. "This whole thing came to a head two weeks ago when he came home, got drunk, yelled at the kids, and then we got in a big fight. Then he wanted to have make-up sex, even though we hadn't made up. My knee-jerk reaction was to take the kids and leave, which we did the next day. But our whole life is in that house and in that town and my mother-in-law's house is a half hour away. I need to figure out how to get him out so we can move back in."

"Pack up his stuff while he is at work, leave it on the sidewalk, and then change all the locks," Shari suggested. "That works. I saw it in some '80s movie."

"The one with Rob Lowe?" exclaimed Becca. "I loved that movie! He's aging nicely, don't you think?"

"I would totally do him," said Shari. "And he's our age so it wouldn't even be gross like if I was hot for some eighteen-year-old teen idol."

Lori and I stared incredulously at Becca and Shari.

"Okay, you two are cut off," I ordered. "No more mojitos for you today."

"Fine. I was ready to switch to a beer anyway," said Shari.

"That's a safe choice," said Becca. "Remember, 'Beer before liquor, never sicker. Liquor before beer, never fear.'" We all laughed, recalling the ditty that guided us safely through many years of binge drinking in college.

I looked down and noticed the menus still on the table. When we had gotten Lori's news, we immediately ordered a round of drinks, but had forgotten to order the food. I thought we should probably all eat something or there would be twelve forgotten kids at their various schools sitting around for hours after dismissal waiting for their fun-loving mothers to pick them up.

"Let's order before we get too stupid," I suggested.

"Too late for that." Shari laughed.

"What can you eat on Jenny Craig, Tracy?" asked Becca, surveying the menu on my behalf.

"I can get a salad and some veggies. I have my own salad dressing and this delicious Anytime bar," I said sarcastically, whipping the tiny bar out of my bag and holding it up.

"Why do they call it an *Anytime* bar?" wondered Shari.

"'Cuz you can eat it anytime," I said. "But only one time a day."

"Then they should call it a *Onetime* bar," she commented.

"Don't get me started on that," I retorted.

We looked over the menus, flagged down the waitress, and ordered. Then I turned to Lori.

"So how are you doing . . . really?"

She took a big swig of her mojito.

"Lousy," she finally admitted. "I thought marriage was forever, you know? I thought having kids would make us stronger. I thought being a mom would make me happy. I'm down three for three." She sighed.

"You *do* love being a mom," I reminded her. "We all do."

"I love my kids. I'm not sure I love being a mom. There's a difference," she said, speaking the unspoken truth most of us felt but were afraid to say out loud.

Although my marriage wasn't disintegrating like Lori's, I could completely relate to her feelings about motherhood. I loved my two children, and while being a mother was not without its rewards, motherhood itself was exhausting. In a way, it was a lot like doing laundry. As soon as you got it done, you immediately had more to do, so you never really got a chance to feel good about the laundry you had just gotten done. This is not to say being a mom was a chore all the time. But oftentimes when I was doing the laundry, I'd think about all the other things I'd rather be doing with my time and it infuriated me. I would be lying if I said I enjoyed every moment I was with the kids and wasn't sometimes thinking about being on a beach in Bali, alone, with a frosty umbrella drink instead.

Knowing that the time when the kids are young is fleeting and it wouldn't be long before they preferred the company of friends to me, I tried to be present and involved when we played Mermaid Barbie meets Ursula the Sea Witch for the sixteen millionth time, understanding when my daughter clung to my leg sobbing when I tried to drop her off at school *every* day, and attentive when the kids told me a story about something that happened at school and the story took ten times longer to tell than it actually happened in real life. I wondered, as I did so often these days, if I had something else to do besides just being a mom, would it make me more appreciative of being a mom and value the time I spent with the kids more?

Truly the best part of being a mom was playing with the kids (tedious as the Adventures of Mermaid Barbie were), or seeing the delight on their faces when they discovered something new and wondrous, or opening a card on Mother's Day with a little, multicolored handprint on the cover and a love note scrawled inside. It was all the stuff in between those moments—the tantrums and bedtime battles, the schlepping the kids along on every errand, the endless amount of cleaning clothes, house, and kids—that made me wonder if there was anyone on the planet who did all this, and only this, and felt fulfilled.

"I hear you," I finally responded to Lori. "I think the problem is we've been sold this bill of goods that being a mom is supposed to be all we need to be content. Maybe it's only supposed to be part of what we need."

"So what else do you think we need?" she asked.

It was the hundred-thousand-dollar question. I thought if I could answer it, I'd not only solve all my own issues but probably a bazillion other women's as well.

"I know what we need," said Shari. "We need more mojitos."

Chapter 17

In New Jersey, Mall Is Spelled "M-A-W-L"

Soon after my lunch with the girls, I realized the time had come for something major. It was something I had been dreading to do, but knew in my heart that I had to do it.

It was time to go bathing suit shopping.

No matter how successful you are on an exercise and diet regimen, I don't think there is any time in a woman's life, after she has had children, when she looks forward to shopping for bathing suits. If there is a hell, I'm pretty sure it would look like a swimsuit department with endless rows of three-way mirrors, skinny salesgirls, and no sarongs.

Even before I had kids, I was never a big fan of bathing suit shopping. Bathing suits are the antithesis of my whole shopping philosophy: I look for clothing that covers up my bad parts and enhances my good parts. Most bathing suits cover nothing except those parts that are illegal to expose on public beaches.

I always got a kick out of those suits that say they give you the "best coverage" in the places you need it most. For most of the women I know, the places we need it most *start* where the bathing suit ends. Honestly, though, I think it's less an issue of my body type and more an issue of timing: Had I lived during the 1940s, the bathing suits would be perfect for me.

Before you have kids, you can go to the beach and stay covered up and no one ever has to see those parts of you that you would rather not be seen in the light of day, outside your bathroom, or by someone who also gives you a cervical exam once a year. When your kids are older and they can swim on their own, you can stay on the beach and watch from afar to make sure they don't drown or pee in the pool or do anything else that will get you in trouble. But when you have little kids, there's no getting around the fact that you're going to have to go in the water . . . and going in the water necessitates the wearing of a bathing suit. This is really unfortunate because the time when your kids are little is when you're in the worst possible shape to wear a bathing suit. It's like some cruel joke by the cellulite gods. When you're a baby and you have dimpled thighs, it is adorable. When you're the mother of the baby and you have the same dimpled thighs, it's not nearly as cute.

I decided I needed some emotional support for this task, so I called my friend Lori. I thought she was the right person for the job even though she was thinner than I was, about three sizes smaller, and had nary a stretch mark or butt dimple to speak of.

"Hey, wanna go to the mall with me?" I asked. She and her husband had switched places: She was back in her house and her husband was at his mother's. Her mother-in-law told Lori she had preferred it the other way around.

"Are we shopping for something or are we just looking for a place to let the kids run wild and pretend we don't see them fishing money out of the fountains?" she wondered.

"I need a bathing suit," I admitted.

"I'm sorry, I just can't be a party to that kind of sadistic torture."

"Bathing suit season is almost upon us and I don't have anything that fits. My suits are all either too small or look like I stole them off of a circus elephant," I whined.

"So you are planning to actually go *on* the beach this summer?"

"I promised Joel I would go back on the beach when the kids were out of those swimmy diapers that inflate like blowfish when they get wet and then explode in a massive shower of pee and absorbent diaper crystals."

"That was a dumb thing to promise," she said.

"I know. I thought I would be thin by the time they were out of diapers."

"You should have told him you meant adult diapers."

"Whatever. Can you come with me or not?"

"I can't. I'm sorry. I'm waiting for the cable guy to come and fix my modem."

I cleared my throat. "Is that like a euphemism for something?"

"Huh?"

"Do you need to be 'serviced'?" I wondered.

"Oh gross!" she exclaimed. "Have you seen the cable guys? They usually look about eight months pregnant and smell like Eau de BO. My electrician, on the other hand . . ."

"Oh, does he *turn you on*?" I snorted.

"Ha-ha!" She laughed. "I think you have been watching

too many Lifetime movies. Divorced women, or almost divorced women such as myself, do not have sordid affairs with their electricians, or anyone else for that matter."

"Maybe they should," I said. "Maybe it would help them get over their asshole almost ex-husbands and feel sexy again."

"That's possible," she agreed. "However, even if I were interested, I don't think my electrician would be. The last time he saw me I was about to give birth on our living room rug."

"Yeah, that could be a vibe killer."

"Besides, I don't even think he knows I'm separated."

"Blow a fuse in your circuit breaker, put on something hot, and call him over."

"I just might do that."

"And think of me pathetically squeezing my massive thighs into a tankini while you wrap your thighs around your electrician dude."

"I think I'll pass."

. . .

I tried three more friends, but no one was available to come bathing suit shopping with me. I suspected most of them probably were free, they just invented excuses so they didn't have to witness my meltdown when I realized there was no bathing suit on the face of the Earth that would cover me from my ass to my elbows and I was going to have to move to Lancaster, Pennsylvania, and join an Amish sect to escape the humiliation of bathing suit season. Unfortunately I had to pick the kids up from school in two hours, which didn't really leave me enough time to get to Lancaster and back, so I sucked it up and went to the mall alone.

Although my thighs were less dimpled than before I started

spinning, they still bore an uncanny resemblance to the man in the moon. There was no disguising this with a bathing suit, so I focused on the parts of me that could be helped. Clearly a bikini was out, and all the one-pieces that hid my bad parts looked like they should have matching rubber, floral bathing caps and come with a free pack of Depends. For someone with a less-than-taut post-baby belly, I thought a tankini with a cute sarong would be my best option. The young salesgirl thought otherwise. She not-so-subtly steered me away from the tankinis to the rack of "Miracle" suits.

"These will make you look ten pounds thinner instantly," she confided in me, as though she came up with the slogan herself. I had actually tried on one of these suits a couple of years earlier and had discovered that although they did make me look ten pounds thinner *around the middle*, all that fat had to go somewhere, which meant it got pushed up or down and over the confines of my bathing suit so I ended up looking twenty pounds heavier everywhere else.

"If I sit next to someone on the beach who is fatter than me, I will look ten pounds thinner instantly, as well," I joked.

She gave me the blank stare of someone who clearly had never experienced the wonders of cellulite and also clearly had never been bigger than a size zero, which, I suspected, also happened to be her IQ.

"Yes," she said, "but if there are no fat people around, you will feel confident in this suit, which will hold in your sagging tummy *and* is also more age appropriate for you than a tankini."

I was floored. I took double offense at the dig to both my body and my horribly advanced age of thirty-six. I could feel bad enough about myself, by myself, without having some skinny, young, idiot salesgirl help me along. Of course I'm sure I was redirecting some of my negative self-image anger at the salesgirl. But when she took away the cute little sarong I was holding and handed me a full-body muumuu instead, I decided she had earned every ounce of my wrath.

"Well, since I'm still a few years away from the retirement home, I think a tankini would be fine for my age," I retorted. "I also think I'd prefer a bathing suit that does not have its own boobs built in, has its own skirt attached, and looks like someone vomited pastel-colored palm trees all over it."

"Um. Okay," she said. She stood with the muumuu still offered, apparently not quite sure if her help was still needed.

"And a word of advice," I told her. "Don't offer a muumuu to a woman with raging post-baby hormones or she might tie you up in it and leave you buried under a mountain of Spanx."

"Oh. Okay. Thanks!" she said brightly. "By the way, my name is Ashley! Let them know I helped you at the register!"

Yeah. Fat chance.

*   *   *

Although Ashley didn't think I was tankini material, Jenny Craig did. According to Jenny's scale, I had lost nine pounds and even though I didn't see a huge difference in the way my clothes fit, I was still confident that I would see an improvement in my bathing suit appearance.

After ditching Ashley, I gathered up a few suits that I thought might hide some sins and play up those parts of me that had not dropped to the floor following the birth of my two children. As I tried on one of the suits in the dressing room I was dismayed to realize that the dressing room had no mirror. Peeking out from the dressing room door, I saw that there was one communal mirror at the end of the hall. I decided that whoever had designed this setup must have either been a man or insane because no woman in her right mind would expect another woman to leave the safety of her dressing room in a bathing suit department to see what she looked like in a public mirror. However, since I could not get a good idea of how I looked by holding my compact mirror up to my butt, I realized I was going to have to risk the ridicule to get a look in the hallway mirror.

Checking to see if the coast was clear, I dashed out and struck a pose in the three-way mirror. This is when I realized Jenny Craig had made a terrible mistake. As I took in my rear view in the three-way mirror, I saw that I had not actually lost nine pounds. It had all just moved around to my backside. There it was, spilling out on all sides from the bathing suit like an escapee from cellulite prison. This was not a rotund rear or even a bodacious backside. This was one big, fat ass. It was the mother of all tushes. It was Buttzilla.

I gasped and grabbed the nearest sarong to wrap around my body. Hearing my cries of horror, another salesclerk ran over.

"Is everything okay?" she asked.

"No. Not okay," I cried. "I had no idea that things were so bad back there."

"Back where?"

I pointed to my other end. "There!"

"Well, maybe it's just the bathing suit you have on. We can find you another," she suggested.

"Do you have one that goes down to my knees?" I asked.

She smiled. "I'm sure it's not as bad as you think," she said diplomatically.

"It is. No. Actually it's worse. It's like someone molded my butt out of Play-Doh and then rolled a bunch of golf balls across it."

I really was shocked. The last time I had looked at my butt was in the '90s and it had been much cuter and tighter and rounder. Of course that was before I had kids and ate my way through a decade of doughnuts.

Since there was no way I could get that butt in shape before bathing suit season and since I was fairly certain that large, lumpy butts were not going to be the new trend this summer, I opted for the bathing suit that looked good from the front, and the longest matching sarong I could find without looking like a member of an Orthodox Jewish sect. I cursed Ashley under my breath for her correct assessment of the situation and then paid an obscene amount of money for this insult to my self-image. Then I took some deep, cleansing breaths and decided that instead of focusing on the bad parts, I should be happy for the progress I had made, the weight I had lost, and the better shape I was in than I was six months ago. I also realized that as bad as I felt, there was a positive light at the end of the tunnel:

Ski season.

• • •

Since I was still in the department store and I wasn't trauma-tized enough by the bathing suit experience, I decided to go down to the jeans department and rub some salt in my wounds. Pretty much every pair of post-baby jeans I had fell clearly into the "mom jeans" category. It's not that I wanted to wear mom jeans. No one in their right mind would purposely seek out a look that makes your butt appear ten times larger than it actually is. But since it was the only style that fit my body for a while, that's what I was stuck wearing. However, now that I was no longer immediately "post-baby" and there was a chance I could wear a normal pair of jeans without looking like knockwurst, I decided to check out the latest look in jeans. Unfortunately for me, the latest style was "skinny jeans." This was not even a particularly good look for anorexics, much less someone who still looked like she could be pregnant from the thighs down.

I thought it highly unlikely that given the skinny style, I could even find a pair of these jeans in my size. I was stunned to discover though, that even skinny jeans come in large sizes. This just goes to prove my theory that manufacturers will make anything for anyone who wants to spend money on it, but just because you can wear something doesn't mean you should.

Optimistically, I pulled a couple of pairs of skinny jeans off the racks in the biggest sizes they had. The girls in the ads all looked great in their skinny jeans tucked into their boots with long t-shirts and oversized sweaters. This is how I envisioned myself looking in the same outfit. However, I could not actually see if this is how I would look in the same outfit because I couldn't even get the damn jeans up past my calves. Apparently, the skinniest part of the skinny jeans is down near your ankles, which for me, was one of the parts where I had gotten bigger when I was pregnant, and stayed that way. All the tags said they were "stretch" jeans, but even stretchy material has its limits. Unless the jeans were made of Flubber, they weren't going to get over my calves.

I worked my way through the skinnies, to the straight legs, on to the boot cuts, and then the flares. At one point there were two-dozen discarded jeans in a heap in my dressing room and one pair in the "keep" pile. The keep jeans were there not because they looked particularly good but because they fit, which was not something I could say about the other two dozen.

While I optimistically struggled to get the last pair on, I heard two women talking loudly in the dressing room next to me.

"Oh. My. Gawd. Yaw butt looks so good in those jeans!" exclaimed a very enthusiastic female voice with a distinctive New Jersey accent. "You *haff* to buy them!"

"I yam gonna buy them," assured the other female New Jersey voice. "And I'm gonna wear them tonight when we go see *National Treashuh*."

I grimaced in my dressing room. Maybe I was more sensitive to it because of the trauma of my bathing suit ordeal, but I was finding the New Jersey–fication of the English language to be completely unbearable. When we had moved to the suburbs, there were two things I couldn't stand: conversations about cleaning products, and New Jersey accents. Since we had, in fact, moved to the suburbs of *New Jersey* and everyone I met was fascinated with cleaning products, you can see how this might have been a poor choice of locations for us to relocate to.

"*Tre-shurrre!*" I bellowed from my dressing room with my jeans around my ankles. "There's an 'R' in it!"

I heard stunned silence next door. I realized I might have overstepped my bounds, but between the bathing suit trauma, jeans nightmare, and now the dueling New Jersey accents, I had hit the wall.

"What's with huh?" asked NJ #1.

"I dunno," responded NJ #2. "Maybe she's havin' a seishuh!"

"See-shurrre!" I bellowed. "There's an 'R' in it!!"

Silence.

"Lady, you have *issues!*" yelled one of the New Jersey girls back at me.

"Fuhget huh," said the other. "Let's go upstairs and look at tankinis."

"Make sure to ask for Ashley," I yelled.

Chapter 18

You Are What You Drive, Especially If It's a Big Car with a Huge Rear End

On the road to a new me, I knew I needed a car to get me there. I always thought that the car I would end up driving when we relocated to the suburbs would be a reflection of my inner coolness. It would be something that said "Hot Mama" or at the very least "Tepid Suburbanite." So when the car we bought from my parents finally coughed up its last carburetor plug, I saw it as opportunity to get something that would tell the world I was a real rebel mom.

Unfortunately, I did not have a great car history to draw from.

I inherited my first car from my older brother. It was a Ford Pinto. If you do not remember this car, it's probably because it was recalled a couple of years after production for the "alleged," ill-fated problem of exploding into a ball of flames when rear-ended. I think my parents knew this when they bought the used Pinto for my brother and then passed it down to me, but they decided to get it anyway because they got a great price on it and, on the off chance something happened, they realized they could save a lot of money on future car insurance to cover us.

To add insult to injury, it was a puke-alicious color green.

It lasted one winter with me before it joined its brethren in Pinto heaven. Butt ugly and dangerous as it was, it had still gotten me from point A to point B, and without a car, I was stranded. I convinced my parents that I needed a car to get home from college and if they got me something new that was a normal color and wasn't condemned by the National Highway Traffic Safety Administration, I would visit more often. My upgrade was a Plymouth Horizon. I thought I was being so chic by getting it in black, but when my dad decided it wasn't worth the money to put in air-conditioning, I quickly learned that a black car without AC heats up faster than a convection oven—and I was the Oven Stuffer Roaster cooking in it. The only good part about that purchase was the fact that I dropped about ten pounds in sheer sweat while I owned it.

After the Plymouth, I graduated college and moved into New York City, at which point I abandoned the idea of having a car. Maybe it's just me, but I thought it would be wiser to use what little money I earned to eat rather than park a car. Ten years later I was back full circle to a butt-ugly used car, which, fortunately, did not explode upon impact, although it probably would have improved its appearance if it did.

Now that I was a big girl and we could afford our own car, I decided the time had finally come to get a car that was in alignment with my image of who I was.

The car dealers were in complete agreement. Which is why they all tried to sell me a minivan.

Minivans, in case you were not really sure, are not cool. I don't think it's a coincidence that a minivan resembles a huge pregnant woman. When the doors slide open and the children emerge, it's just like childbirth . . . except, you know, minus all the screaming and hemorrhoids. I'm convinced this was all a grand marketing scheme by the minivan design teams to subliminally appeal to the maternal instincts of the suburban moms. What mom wouldn't want to drive a car that looks . . . like a mom? Me, for one. I saw it as the great suburban sellout. Truth be told, I wanted a motorcycle, but I just could not fathom how to get two car seats onto the back of a Harley.

"This is our newest model!" boasted Pete, the car salesman, as he guided us to the center of the showroom. I was optimistic that this was going to be a very quick process. After doing a month of research and weighing the pros and cons of a number of car styles, we had ultimately decided on a midsized SUV. While it was not as cool as a motorcycle or a convertible, it did have the ability to actually haul me, the kids, and all their stuff around, and was not as egregious in my mind as driving a minivan. By the time we went out to test drive some cars, I had a pretty good idea of what we should get.

But apparently Pete thought otherwise.

"It's a minivan," I said, glaring at the monster car with the biggest rear end I had ever seen on an inanimate object.

"We don't call it that," he responded.

"But that's what it is," I argued.

"Technically, yes. But we see it as a *luxury family vehicle*."

"Call it what you want . . . it's a minivan any way you slice it."

"Why don't we just check it out, honey?" suggested my husband. "It looks very roomy."

"If I wanted roomy, I'd get a tank. At least those have some attitude. This just screams *suburbanite*." I looked at the huge back end of the minivan again. "*Fat* suburbanite."

Pete smiled patiently. I got the feeling I was not the first reluctant mom he had encountered. But he had no idea what he was up against this time. I was a woman with a mission and that mission did not include purchasing and driving around a massive mom-mobile.

With the flourish of a third-rate bar mitzvah magician, Pete pressed a button on the key and the car honked and the headlights flashed.

"Helps you find the car in the mall parking lot!" He winked at me. I rolled my eyes. I would need a SWAT team to find my minivan in the sea of ten thousand other honking and flashing minivans in the mall parking lot.

He pressed another button and the doors unlocked. He opened the passenger door and my kids ran over and climbed in.

"This is the best part," he said as he pressed another button and the back passenger door slid open. "The kids won't bang the door into other cars and you can open and close it right from the driver's seat."

As the door finished sliding open, my kids jumped out of the minivan.

"I'm having flashbacks to giving birth," I commented.

"There is an integrated DVD system," he added.

"*Yay!*" yelled my kids.

"Does it come with a fast pass for the McDonald's drive-through?" I asked contemptuously.

"No, but there is an optional refrigeration unit you can install for an additional cost through the dealership to keep the kids' snacks cold!"

"Is it big enough to hide a dead body in?" I wondered.

He smiled nervously at me. My husband elbowed me in the ribs.

"And we happen to have one left on the lot in *titanium* that you can drive home today!" he exclaimed, directly to me.

"They make minivans out of titanium now?" I asked. "Will it shield us from Kryptonite?"

"Titanium is the color," said Pete.

"Oooh, titaniummmm!" My son nearly swooned. Five minutes after we had gotten him a very expensive handheld video game for Hanukkah, they had come out with a new model in "titanium" and he had been pleading for it ever since. It had the exact same functionality as the one he already owned, but everyone, even a five-year-old, knows everything is much cooler in titanium.

"Of course, if you're not a fan of titanium, I'm sure we can find another color you would like," he said to me. Then he turned to my husband. "The ladies are all about the DVD system and the color of the car!" He winked at my husband.

Truth be told, it didn't matter to me what color the car came in, because when he said this, all I saw was red.

I narrowed my eyes at him and said nothing for a moment. My husband inhaled sharply and then took a step back and waited for the tsunami to hit.

"There's a reason for that," I finally said to Pete. "As women, our heads are so stuffed with things like how to keep the floors clean, what to cook our family for dinner, and how to get their whites their brightest white, that we don't have any more room in our brains for things like politics, the economy, and car specifications."

He squinted his eyes at me, trying to decide if I was serious or not.

"And then there's the issue of PMS," I continued. "It clouds our brains to such an extent that we can't possibly focus on things like fuel economy and front-wheel versus rear-wheel drive."

He looked at my husband for help. My husband shrugged and said nothing. It's a wise man who knows to stay silent when his wife is in the throes of an angry tirade.

"Besides," I continued. "Women are so one-dimensional that you know we really can't think of anything more important when purchasing a car than what color it comes in. Who can think about things like side curtain air bags and safety ratings when you have the grueling decision to make between a black interior versus a beige interior?"

He gave a nervous little laugh.

"So, Pete, thanks for reminding me how lucky I am to have you and my husband here to help us make sure we get a safe, reliable car, because even though I graduated college with honors and have an IQ of 148, which is probably double yours, I'm sure I couldn't even begin to understand such complex issues as gas mileage and air bags."

I smiled brightly at him. He moved his lips but no words came out.

"Give us a second, Pete," said my husband, grasping my arm. He threw some candy at the kids to occupy them and then pulled me off to the side.

"I know what you're going to say," I huffed.

"This is not about the color of the car or the stupid car salesman," he said.

"He's an idiot," I sneered.

"Yes, he's an idiot. But the only reason you let him get to you is because you hate the idea of a minivan."

"Luxury family vehicle," I corrected him.

"Yeah, whatever. But can you open your mind a little and consider it? It is incredibly convenient and I think it will make your life easier."

"Unless it will clean up the house, feed the kids, and pick up your dry cleaning for me, it really doesn't make my life that much easier," I said. "Honestly, I'd rather get out and open my own damn door than drive around in a minivan, regardless of what color it is.

"And by the way," I continued, "did you notice that he was so busy talking about the doors and the DVD system, he didn't mention the gas mileage? I looked it up. It gets eleven miles to the gallon in the city. *Eleven!* Our neighbor's RV got better gas mileage than that and he could go to the bathroom in his car!"

"I bet there is an optional toilet you can install in the mini-van for an additional cost through the dealership," he said, mimicking the salesman.

"Screw that. I'll just bring the kids' potty with me on long car rides."

"So, what do you say?" he coaxed. "Humor me. Let's take it for a test drive. Then we'll go out and get some iced espressos!"

I nodded reluctantly and immediately cursed myself for selling my soul for an iced coffee.

Pete made copies of our driver's licenses and then ushered us outside to the test-drive model. We buckled the kids into the integrated car seats, popped in a Disney DVD for them, and then I jumped into the driver seat. As I eased the car out of the dealership I wondered if I would need to get a captain's license because it felt like I was steering a cruise ship.

"What do you think, honey?" asked my husband from back in the third row.

"What did you say?" I yelled back to him. "I can't hear you. There are two kids, a lion singing, and about forty miles of minivan between us!"

I joined the throngs of minivans already on the road and pulled into a lane behind a clone of the car we were driving. The back of the car had a "Baby on Board" sign in the window, a large "Disney Family" decal on the bumper, and a sticker of stick figures made up of a mom, a dad, about ten kids, a dog, and a cat. I was surprised with that number of kids that the mom was driving a minivan and not a school bus. Through the rear window, I could see an animated movie playing on their DVD system as well.

Feeling panic welling up inside me like a bad case of indigestion, I stepped on the gas and moved to the left of the other minivan to pass it. I decided that my son's matchbox cars accelerated faster than the minivan I was driving. As I came up parallel with the other minivan, I looked to my right to see who was driving. It was another mom, about my age, with her hair tucked under a baseball cap . . . that sported mouse ears. Hanging from her rearview mirror was a pair of fuzzy dice . . . with mouse ears. I looked up at the roof to see if the car itself was equipped with a pair of mouse ears (installed at an additional cost by the dealership). Just as I was about to pull ahead and pass, the other mom turned her head and looked at me, gave me a giant, orthodontic-filled grin, and then shot me a big thumbs-up.

I turned and yelled back to my husband.

"We are *not* getting a minivan!"

· · ·

"I'm not getting a minivan," I said again as I stood at the kitchen counter making dinner.

"Yes, I got that," my husband sighed. "You mentioned it about a dozen times."

"I just wanted to make sure I was clear about that."

"Very clear," he said. "But can I ask you something?"

"What?"

"Why does it matter what you drive?" he wondered. "Who's gonna care? The other moms? They all drive them, too. You think when any woman is a little girl she thinks, 'Someday when I grow up and I become a mommy, I'm gonna drive a minivan!' No. You do it because your life is crazy complicated being a mother and you do whatever you need to do to make things just a little bit simpler. And if that includes driving a minivan . . . in *titanium* . . . you do it."

I put down the chopping knife, came around the counter, and sat down on a stool across from him.

"I hear what you are saying," I admitted. "But I guess I'd rather be a little inconvenienced than feel like I had traded every aspect of my life for all the uncool manifestations of motherhood."

"But you are a mother," he argued. "Why are you fighting it so hard?"

"I'm not fighting being a mother. I'm fighting *looking* like a mother."

"Why does that matter?" he repeated.

I sighed. "I used to define myself completely by how I

looked and what I did for a living. I don't have a job to define myself by anymore—or at least not a paying job—and even though everyone says motherhood is the most important job you can have, it's kind of bullshit because people who do have paying jobs do not respect women who don't."

I paused and looked around at all the kid chaos in the house. If ever there was a vision of the manifestations of motherhood, it was the toy explosion that was my living room.

"I've spent a lot of time learning to be okay with my choices and not devalue what I do just because other people do," I explained. "But along the way I realized that one of the reasons a lot of people look down on moms is because the second we become moms we start to let ourselves go. We do what's easy and what's comfortable and we give up our individuality. Part of that's necessary because kids are messy and you have to put their needs first. But I don't think you have to completely lose yourself in motherhood. And for me, part of holding on to who I am is not driving a big, pregnant car."

"What if we got some fuzzy dice with mouse ears to go on your mirror?" He grinned.

"Oh my God! You saw that, too?"

He nodded and laughed.

"Honey, I'm not going to make you do anything you don't want to do," he said softly. "But maybe it's time to let go of all the expectations of how you think this is all supposed to go and just do what feels right to you." He took my face in his hands and planted a big kiss on my forehead. I finally got the sense that one of us was definitely beginning to unravel the mystery of what I needed to be happy. I was just hoping it was me.

Chapter 19

~~~~~~~~~~

I Work, Therefore I Am

"You know, you're really looking great!" my husband exclaimed.

I looked at my reflection in the mirror and tried to see what my husband was seeing. My eyes came to rest on a generous pair of thighs that would make Frank Perdue salivate.

"I'm not quite there yet," I said critically.

"Maybe not," he said, coming up and hugging me from behind. "But you have to feel good about what you have accomplished so far."

I did actually. I had lost fifteen pounds over six months by exercising and eating Jenny Craig . . . although I suspected that at least five of those pounds were pure gas. My back pains and stomach cramps were better and my headaches were gone, due probably to a combination of exercise, psychotherapy, and antidepressants. Although I didn't need someone with a PhD to tell me that I was going through an identity crisis, it helped to have someone listen objectively while I spent an hour each week talking about why giving up my career had thrown me into a mental Tilt-a-Whirl. Fortunately, my new therapist did not seem to have a penchant for cosmetic surgery and actually focused on what I was saying rather than her own aging issues and peeling face.

It was no revelation to me that I defined myself by what I did and how I looked and assumed other people did, too. It was a little bit of a chicken or egg thing, though. I'm not sure if I enjoyed my career *because* other people thought it was cool and I got lots of positive feedback from it, or if it was something I really just enjoyed doing *and* I liked that people thought it was cool. I tend to think it was more the former than the latter because I was actually happy when I quit my job and felt a strange sense of relief not to have to do it anymore . . . until I realized that now all I had to go on for external validation were my mommying skills. What I got from the therapy was the realization that it's okay to enjoy getting positive feedback from people for the things that I do, as long as it's not the *only* reason I do things. It's human nature to want people to admire you. I'm pretty sure that anyone who says they don't care what other people think of them is full of crap. However, there is a difference between living your life and living your life for the approval of others. By the time I had quit my job, I definitely wasn't enjoying it anymore, but I was still getting a lot of external validation for doing it, and for me, that was a really hard thing to give up and live without.

While the haircut and weight loss and all that helped with the externals, and the therapy and drugs helped with the internals, I still needed to address my desire to have a purpose. Wanting to have something that you do, that is all your own and gives you a sense of satisfaction from doing it, is not a bad thing. But from the reaction I got from a lot of people when I told them I needed a purpose, you'd think I had suggested becoming a drug dealer. They would tsk-tsk and say that I *had* a purpose: It was to take care of my family and raise two children to be happy, healthy, independent people. That was *a* purpose, and certainly my most important job. But for me, it couldn't be the only thing I looked forward to when I woke up each day. In the same breath, I didn't want to go to a job every day and have someone else raise my kids. I had tried that briefly and I was miserable. As hard as parenting was sometimes, I wanted to be the one they remembered teaching them to tie their shoelaces, read a Dr. Seuss book, and burp on command.

"I am happy that I'm getting back in shape and can wear my cool clothes again. Although my cool clothes from five years ago are surprisingly not so cool anymore," I complained.

"Hold on to them for ten more years and then they'll be cool again," said my husband.

"True that. But in the meantime, I still need to buy some new clothes. All I have are fat clothes and acid-washed jeans."

"Okay, but go easy, all right? Things are a little tight right now."

"Tight how?" I wondered.

"Tight, money tight. It's been slow. This is the downside to having your own business and not getting a steady paycheck."

I grimaced. "I'm sorry. I feel bad about spending money on stupid stuff when I'm not contributing financially."

"You are contributing. You're saving us the cost of a housekeeper and a nanny."

"Oh great." I sighed. "Thanks."

"No. I mean, of course you're worth much more to us than that, but those are our cost savings by having you home."

"So my life insurance policy just covers me for the cost of child care and cleaning?"

"Pretty much."

"Thanks for that boost to my self-image."

He gave me a squeeze. "I've got to get to work."

"Yeah, me, too. I have kids to care for and a house to clean."

The conversation with my husband was another reminder to me that I still felt this gaping hole where my career used to be. With one kid in elementary school and the other in preschool, it seemed like a good time to start exploring some options. However, finding a job for three days a week, three hours a day was a tough order to fill unless I entered the world of suburban prostitution.

A lot of my friends had started to work part-time by going into home-based businesses. But much as I loved clothes and accessories, I couldn't see myself going house-to-house to hold belt, bag, and blouse parties, or hawking high-end kitchen gadgets, superior antiaging serums, or any of the other multitudes of exclusive home-sold goods that you're told you can't live without, but somehow I have managed to. My thought is, if I've lived thirty-some-odd years without spending $175 on cow placenta cream for my fine lines and wrinkles, I'm not going to ask my friends to do it just so I can get twenty percent off my next purchase of lip plumper. This is not to say I didn't enjoy going to some of these parties and I had a lot of friends who did really well financially by hosting them. But it wasn't for me.

Some other moms I knew went to work part-time for their husbands doing clerical jobs and bookkeeping. Sadly, this was not part of my skill set. If I did the bookkeeping, we'd be bankrupt in a week. As for my filing skills, they were limited to my fingernails. Besides, if my husband and I spent every day together working at his music studio, it would be either the end of his business, the end of our marriage, or both. It's not that I didn't love him desperately, utterly, and absolutely. From the moment we met at the entrance to a recording studio where he was the new manager and I was a young TV producer, it was love at first sight . . . for me, anyway. Once I decided he was the man I was meant to marry, it was just a matter of time before he came around, dumped the blonde floozy he was dating, and fell in love with me. We were a great team in every way, but working together was out of the question. He was the boss at his office. I was the boss at home. If I came to his office and had to be subservient to the boss, I would probably kill him. Of course, I didn't know this for sure, but I didn't want to take the chance and then end up leaving my children fatherless.

There were lots of advertisements for businesses that said you could work your own hours and make lots of money at home. But making annoying sales calls did not seem like something that would feel either mentally stimulating or beneficial to society. It felt like something that would eventually cause me to either shoot myself or be shot by someone else.

As an alternative to a paid job, many of my friends had gotten very involved in volunteering for one cause or another. While their work was admirable and I'm sure it was very satisfying, even they said it often felt like the volunteering was a full-time job itself, but without the paycheck. Plus, the sheer number of places that wanted my time/money/attention was completely overwhelming. For every well-known charitable organization, there were ten more I'd never heard of and honestly, I just couldn't see myself helping plan a canine cotillion for dogs with ADHD, or collecting gently used shells for homeless turtles.

Finally, there were the moms who thought staying home with their kids was a great opportunity to improve their backhand or their shopping skills. It's nice that it worked for them, but I'd have far too much Jewish guilt to let my husband work his ass off while I played a set of doubles, had a two-hour Bloody Mary lunch with the girls to talk about our interior decorators, and then went shopping at the mall. When your kids are little and you barely have time for a shower while they are in preschool, I think it's every mom for herself and if you want to spend that two hours at the mall, you have earned that right. But by the time your kids are in school all day, every day, I think you should find a way to contribute to society in some way other than looking at swatches for the chaises at your new vacation home, or trying to kill your nemesis on the tennis court. But, hey, that's just me.

One thing was for sure, I wasn't going to find a job that suited my schedule and my talents in the newspaper help-wanted section. If I was going to find the perfect job, I was going to have to invent it.

. . .

Life had settled into a comfortable routine of the kids doing kid things, the husband doing husband things, and all the appliances in the house systematically breaking down. If looked at objectively, it all was actually hysterically funny. But I was a little too close to the action to see the absurdity in it at the time. It would take a monumental event to show me the humor in my situation . . . and my new career path. It would take a cataclysmic occurrence. It would take . . . a valentine.

It happened the day I picked my son up from school and he told me excitedly that they would be celebrating Valentine's Day in his class. He said he wanted to bring in valentines for all of his classmates.

I had, what I thought, was a normal, mature reaction to this innocent request.

I panicked.

"What if he doesn't get any valentines back?" I cried to my husband. I thought of how my son's little heart would break if Julia gave a valentine to Gregory, but not to him. If Chris and Ben got a bunch of little pink and red cards from Jessica and Sarah, but my son did not. I knew when it came to girls, my son would sooner kiss a tarantula than a member of the opposite sex. But I also knew that receiving valentines when you are little is not about love. It's about acceptance and belonging. Not getting a valentine is like being the last one picked for kickball. It's like not having someone ask you to be their twin for Twin Day. It's like having to sit with the teacher on the bus when you go on a field trip because in a class of seventeen, sixteen kids paired up and you were left sitting alone.

"It could scar him for the rest of his life," I warned. My husband stared at me and gave me the look he usually gives me when I go off the deep end about something really stupid.

"I'm sure he will do just fine," he said. "He's his father's son, after all."

"So what does that mean? He'll date a bunch of vapid blonde bimbos before he meets a smart, funny brunette and marries her?"

He glared at me. "No. I'm just saying he's a handsome,

charismatic little guy and I'm sure the girls will be falling over themselves to have him be their valentine."

"But what if they don't?"

"Honey, don't you think it's a little neurotic to obsess about the love life of a six-year-old?" he wondered.

"These things can have long-term repercussions. It could affect his ability to be in a committed relationship when he is older," I explained. My husband looked at me skeptically.

"It's true," I insisted. "I saw it on *Dr. Phil.*"

"Call the teacher. I'm sure she has it covered."

Although I was concerned for the emotional well-being of my son and I was willing to express that to my husband, I did not really want the teacher to know I was diving into the deep end of the pool over my son's valentine worthiness. So instead of calling her, I went to the card store and bought chocolate Kisses, heart-shaped lollipops, and little candies with unisex messages on them like "you're neat" and "ooh-la-la." I filled red cellophane bags with the candy and hot-glue-gunned little Power Ranger valentine cards onto each one addressed to each kid in his class. Then I baked a batch of slice-and-cook valentine's cookies and wrote each kid's name with red icing on a cookie.

"Don't you think this is a little over the top?" asked my husband when he saw all the valentine's goodies stacked up on the table. "This looks like Valentine's Day at the Wonka factory."

"No. When the other kids see what our kid is bringing in, they are going to fall all over themselves to give him a damn valentine!"

"So we are teaching him he can *buy* love and acceptance?" asked my husband.

"I see nothing wrong with that," I responded.

While I finished curling the ribbon to tie around the bags, my son walked in and handed me a piece of paper.

"What's this?" I asked him.

"A note from my teacher. I forgot to give it to you yesterday."

I put down the scissors and wiped my icing-covered hands on my pants. Then I looked at the note. The teacher asked us to make sure to buy seventeen valentines and have our child sign each one. She said each child in the class would have their own valentine mailbox and at the class valentine party, they would *each* receive a valentine from all seventeen of their classmates. No one would be left out.

"*Every* kid gets a valentine from everyone in the class?" I wondered aloud.

"Yeah, duh, Mom," said my son. "Otherwise some people like Icky Hillary wouldn't get any."

"Of course," I said dumbly. "I figured that."

He ran off to kill Nazi zombies in some video game and left me staring at an overabundance of cookies and candy with egg on my face.

For about a minute, I felt insanely stupid. Then, I realized the whole thing was insanely funny. I went into the bathroom and washed all the goo off my hands. Then I thought for a minute, walked into our home office, sat down at the computer, and in about fifteen minutes wrote a short story about the whole experience. I hadn't really written much of anything except grocery lists since I had quit my job five years earlier, but the story flowed out of me easily. When it was done, I stared at it and tried to figure out what I was feeling. It occurred to me that what I felt was a great sense of relief that all my creativity hadn't left my body when I gave birth. Apparently, just like the cellulite, it was all still there, just below the surface.

So now what? I was overjoyed in the accomplishment of just doing something purely for me. But I wanted more. While I looked around distractedly trying to figure out what to do next, my eye caught a stack of newspapers on the floor of the office. I recalled that our local paper sometimes ran short opinion pieces written by people in the community. I quickly looked up the e-mail address of the editor of the paper, and before I could change my mind, I dashed off a quick cover letter and sent my essay in.

Two weeks later it was in print.

A week after that, I got a check in the mail.

"Ten bucks!" I yelled, waving the check in front of my husband. "They paid me ten bucks for my column!" I hooted.

"Are we happy about this?" asked my husband who couldn't tell if I was excited or about to call the writers' union and file a complaint.

"Yes!" I exclaimed. "I mean, no, not about the amount. Ten bucks is ridiculous. But I wasn't expecting to get paid anything for that piece. I sent it in as a whim! They didn't hire me to write it. This is like when you get a birthday card from a great aunt you thought was dead and she includes a ten-dollar bill in the card. It's bonus bucks!"

"That's cool, honey!" he exclaimed. "So what's your plan?"

"What'ya mean?"

"Are you going to write more?"

I paused in my revelry. I hadn't actually thought about it. The wheels began to turn in my mind and I realized I might have inadvertently stumbled onto something game changing.

"You think if I wrote some more stories about the kids, the paper would run them?"

"I don't know," he replied. "It worked for Erma Bombeck."

"Yeah, well, I'm no Erma Bombeck."

"You know what, you're pretty funny. And I think a lot of other moms will relate to your experiences," he commented.

"You think other moms almost blow up their houses when they are cooking and have issues trying to be cool in the suburbs?" I wondered.

"What do you think?"

"I guess there are some." I thought for a minute. "I certainly have enough material. And I have time while the kids are in school to write."

"So . . ."

"Okay!" I announced. "I'll write a few more and send them in to the local paper and see if they are interested."

"Great!"

"I actually have an idea for one about you, too!" I said.

"Oh crap."

． ． ．

The paper had gotten a good response to my valentine column so they were willing to try me out once a month when their regular columnist had the week off. In the interim weeks, they asked if I would write some local news stories to help them fill in for some reporters who had left. Somehow they had gotten the impression that I had been a writer for the local TV news, not a writer of *promos* for the local news, which were two vastly different jobs. The news writers were actual journalists. The promo writers were basically advertising copywriters with zero journalistic integrity and even less journalistic experience. However, I'd had no experience delivering singing telegrams in a gorilla suit when I got that job after college so I figured I could fake it and write news articles, too.

My first assignment was an interview with the chief of police of our town. I hoped that he wouldn't recognize my name from various police reports that had been filed over the years having to do with my history driving into snowbanks, committing vehicular garage-door slaughter, and the infamous bathrobe incident. Fortunately, he seemed oblivious to my notoriety and answered my questions about a new emergency response notification system without any suspicion that he was being interviewed by a nefarious suburban scofflaw.

All was going well and then, as we were wrapping up the interview, the chief suddenly paused and peered over my shoulder.

"What?" I asked.

"I think you have something stuck in the hood of your sweatshirt," he told me. As a laundry-challenged mom who had struggled her whole adult life in the war against static cling, I naturally assumed whatever was back there was the result of my latest dryer battle.

"Can I help you?" he asked dangling his hand over my shoulder. I nodded, figuring I had been walking around with an errant sock attached to the back of my head. The chief smiled, reached out, and peeled the item in question from the hood of my sweatshirt.

It was a pair of my thong underwear.

We both froze. He stood there for a full minute trying to formulate some words of apology while he held my thong out in front of him pinched between his index finger and his thumb. I stared at the underwear unable to move while I felt my journalistic credibility fly out the police station window. Finally I broke the silence.

"Oh," I said, as I reached out, grabbed the underwear, and stuffed it in my pocket.

"Those are my husband's."

• • •

Apparently there were a lot of moms reading the newspaper who could relate to my stories about motherhood and feeling lost in suburbia because within six months my monthly column was moved into a weekly slot. Three months after that it was picked up by two more newspapers in the same chain. I was feeling pretty good about having created a new career for myself, and after so many years of feeling utterly lost and unfulfilled, it was incredibly gratifying to have something that I did apart from being a wife and mother that filled me with a sense of purpose and joy. Of course, the money I made was barely enough to cover the cost of the ink I printed my invoices on, but it was something, and I felt good about contributing more than just the money we saved on the cost of a housekeeper, cook, and driver.

The kids understood that I wrote a humor column and that quite often it was about them, but they seemed less interested in what I was writing than the fact that I had my picture in the paper every week and they thought that was neat. This was some years before the explosion of the mommy blogger phenomenon on the Internet where it is generally accepted that you have carte blanche to write about everything that happens in your family, feelings be damned. There were no such rules when I started writing my column and no one who really set the standard for defining the limits of privacy, so it was up to me to figure out how much personal stuff to let fly in my columns. Unfortunately, in the beginning, I wasn't very good at it. Giddy with my public platform and growing fan base, I wrote about *everything*, from my son's questions about the birds and the bees to my daughter's naked Barbie obsession, without giving too much thought to who might be reading it in our town and how that might affect my kids.

Then one week I wrote a column about how my daughter still slept with a blankie. I knew many of the other moms from our school read my column, but it never occurred to me that they might be reading the column to their kids, as well. The day after the column ran in the paper, my daughter came home from school in tears after a number of kids made snarky remarks to her about the fact that she still had a security blanket. It was obvious that she was upset, but I still didn't get the depth of my betrayal until the following week when I met her at school. As the two of us walked through the hallway, another mom saw me and suddenly stopped.

"Are you Tracy Beckerman?" she asked.

"Yes."

"Oh, I have to tell you, I *love* your column. I read it every week. It is *so* funny," she exclaimed.

I beamed at her, eating up the praise and recognition. Out of the corner of my eye I noticed my daughter scowling, but I blinked away her response.

"Thanks so much!" I replied joyfully. The other woman turned and left. I took my daughter's hand and started back down the hallway.

"Another fan for the backstabber," she mumbled under her breath.

"Excuse me?" I said with a start.

"Nuthin'," she muttered.

* * *

"I don't think Emily is happy about my new career," I admitted to my husband later that week as we got ready for bed.

"Why do you say that?"

"Well, after I wrote a column about her sleeping with a blankie, the other kids at school found out and made fun of her."

"I'd be mad if you wrote that about me, too," he admitted.

"If you still slept with a blankie, you'd have bigger things to worry about than me writing about it in the newspaper."

"I just mean I'd be upset if you wrote something personal like that about me."

"Yeah, I know," I said sullenly.

"Just take this as a reminder that you need to put our family before your column," he said seriously. "I'm not saying, don't write about us. I just think you have to consider our privacy and how we will feel if you air all our dirty laundry in public."

"But what if it's funny laundry?" I said.

"Honey, you can make fun of yourself and you can make fun of me, but you need to watch what you write about the kids or they will really start to resent you."

I scowled. "I think they already do. Yesterday I took Emily to the supermarket and while we were waiting on the checkout line, she pointed to one of those trashy celebrity tabloid magazines they have there on the rack and she said, 'Mommy, you look just like the movie stars on the cover of this magazine!'"

"That's sweet," he commented.

"Yeah, I thought so, too. And then I looked at the magazine

and it was covered with a bunch of pictures of ugly butts and the headline said, 'Stars with Cellulite.'"

He burst out laughing. I frowned, and then giggled, too.

"Wow, she's really pissed at you!" he said.

"I know."

"Listen, I'm really glad that you found something that fills a void in your life," he said, sitting me down on the bed and taking my hands in his. "I really am. But you need to look at your reasons for doing it. Are you writing the column because it makes you feel good to write and get paid for your efforts and do something that is not all about cooking and cleaning and being a mom, or are you writing so people will love you and tell you how funny you are and give you a lot of attention?"

"Can't it be a little of both?" I wondered.

"I think you can enjoy the fact that people like reading it and treat you a little bit like a local celebrity. But don't do it just for the external validation. Otherwise you will end up right back where you were five years ago, you know?

"Let the validation come from in here," he added, poking a finger gently into my chest.

"That's deep," I commented.

"You know what I mean," he said.

"But I just put so much time and energy into losing weight, cutting my hair, getting a tattoo, buying non-mom jeans, and creating a cool career." I sighed dramatically. "I kind of feel like Dorothy in *The Wizard of Oz* when Glinda tells her she didn't need to bother following the yellow brick road or melting the wicked witch. She could have gone home anytime just by clicking her stupid ruby slippers."

"What do you mean?"

"Maybe I didn't need to do all this to feel cool," I said,

sweeping my hand back and forth across the front of my body. "Maybe I just needed to click my heels and say, 'I can be happy without a cool job or a cool haircut because it's not about what I do or what I wear or what I drive. It's about who I am as a person.'"

"That's very profound, honey."

"I know." I paused and thought for a minute. Then I shook my head.

"But I still don't think I could be cool in a minivan."

Chapter 20

A Word of Advice: Don't Look for Love from the People You Fired

For people in the TV promo business, the big, go-to event each year is the annual Promax Conference. It's four days of schmoozing and partying, with a little more partying thrown in for good measure. Tickets are cost-prohibitive so you typically have to count on the deep pockets of your employer to send you to represent their company and hopefully not embarrass them by doing things like ripping the seat cover off your hotel bathroom toilet and participating in drunken kickboard races in the pool at three in the morning.

Not that I ever did that.

Once I quit my job and became a stay-at-home mom, there was no one to foot the bill for a Promax pass for me, and really no reason for me to go, anyway. However, as someone who occasionally wrote music for promos and other TV marketing campaigns, my husband had a vested interest in attending the conference and he would spring for his own pass each year. As a newcomer to the column-writing world, I had yet to find my own network of colleagues or attend the writing conferences of my new trade. So, while I was no longer a part of the promo world, I still wasn't really a part of the print world, either, and I felt a twinge of envy each year when my husband would go to the conference and I would stay home to do mommy things.

This time when the conference rolled around again and I prepared for my annual sulk, my husband announced that he had been invited to one of the parties with a "plus one." Although my life had changed dramatically in the six years I had been away from the promo business, I knew that many of the people I had worked with in my past life were still doing the same thing they had been doing, in the same place they had been doing it when I left the industry, and they would all be at this party. My husband thought it would be fun for me to come to the party and reconnect with old friends. I thought it would be a great opportunity to go back and show everyone how awesome I was, without falling back on the "used to be's." I imagined my former associates fighting to talk to me and compliment me and be utterly jealous of the new life I had created for myself. Of course I also imagined that Hollywood would decide to make a movie about my life, pay me a bazillion dollars, and we would move to L.A., buy Johnny Depp's house, and get a pet unicorn—which just shows you what kind of fantasy world I was living in.

After locking in a babysitter, as well as a backup babysitter in case the first one flaked out on us, I decided that even if no one wanted to talk to me, at the very least I was going to look damn good standing in a corner by myself. So I went and got a haircut, a manicure, a pedicure, a facial, an eyebrow shaping, and a full body wax, because nothing says uncool like hair on your big toe.

Next I went to the mall and bought two pairs of Spanx to wear under my dress because one was good, but two would smooth out the bumps caused by the first pair pushing my fat up and over the waistband. This is actually called "double Spanxing" and is a common technique used by new moms and male models over forty.

Finally I decided it wouldn't kill my kids to live on chicken nuggets for a week and I took my grocery money to go get a drop-dead gorgeous dress that was just the right combination of sexy and professional and would hide whatever remaining rolls of fat that had escaped the confines of double Spanx jail.

When the big night arrived, I felt confident and ready.

The party was at a new, uber-hip spot in New York City in Soho. The door was unmarked, save for the red rope on the sidewalk and the stone-faced bouncer in all black guarding the door from anyone who looked tragically unhip or obviously suburban.

Somehow, I passed inspection and made it in.

"I see a couple of people I need to meet," said my husband, whispering into my ear as we pushed some heavy velvet curtains out of the way and entered a blood-red room. "Are you going to be okay or do you need me to stick with you?"

I gave his elbow a squeeze. "I got this," I assured him and myself at the same time.

I immediately spotted a former colleague from my old office and sashayed over to say hello. His eyes met mine and I saw his eyebrows go up in a look of surprise, mixed, I thought, with a tiny bit of annoyance. I flinched inwardly and wondered if I might have made a mistake in coming. TV people liked to be revered by other people, especially other TV people who have fallen down the success ladder. On the surface, I certainly met that criteria. The difference was I had chosen to leave when I was at the *top* of my game, although I'd left for something that appeared to be less impressive than what I used to do. This strange dichotomy made me an unknown entity in a conversation and I could see in my colleague's eyes that he wasn't sure how he was going to play his card.

I grabbed a piece of chicken satay from a passing plate of appetizers and approached him.

"Garry. Hiiii," I said with mock enthusiasm.

"Tracy. Wow! Good to see you," he replied giving me a cool kiss on the air next to my cheek.

"How's the promo business going?" I asked.

"Great. *Great!*" he enthused. "I left Channel 2 and went freelance and I am *insanely* busy."

Clearly he thought I wasn't just living in the suburbs, I was living under a rock. I knew he had been fired. *Everyone* knew he'd been fired. But I played along.

"How about you? Still home with the kids?" he asked with thinly veiled disdain.

"I am," I replied somewhat nervously. I had debated whether to tell everyone about my new career as a humor columnist, but I decided to see if I could make it through the evening with all my self-confidence intact, without dragging out a new job title to define myself. Of course I had shamelessly spent hundreds of dollars to make sure I looked better than I did when I left the business, but that was beside the point.

I was about to ask him about a mutual friend when he suddenly took my arm and pulled me over to the side of the room where several women I didn't know were engaged in conversation.

"I want to introduce you to someone. Tracy, this is my wife, Laura," he said gesturing to a demure-looking brunette with a Mom Bob. "Tracy and I used to work together a hundred years ago," he said to Laura. Then he turned back to me. "Laura is a stay-at-home mom, like you! And these are the wives of some other promo people here. I'm sure you all have a lot in common."

I had wondered what card he would play. Now I realized it was the Trump Card.

Garry grinned deviously at me, gave his wife a peck on the cheek, and walked away. I stood there and seethed and reminded myself how happy I was that I'd had him fired.

I decided to be polite and spend a moment with "the wives." If Garry's reaction was any indication, being with the wives would probably be less unpleasant than hanging out with the promo people, anyway. I was surprised at how badly I had miscalculated my welcome, but thought there were probably other people there whom I hadn't had fired who would greet me with more honest enthusiasm.

Laura introduced me around and then turned to include me in the conversation.

"So, Tracy, where do you live?"

"I'm in New Jersey," I responded.

"Ohhh." The women all nodded their heads and smiled. It was apparent that no one else lived in New Jersey and had nothing to add to a conversation about New Jersey.

"And how old are your kids?" asked another mom whose name I had immediately forgotten.

"Almost five and seven," I replied. "How about yours?"

"I have a nine-month-old and three-year-old twins," said the other mom.

"Twins? Twins are so cool!" said a woman named Nancy.

"It's fun," nodded twin-mom. "But it's definitely double the mess!"

"Oh, you should get these new cleaning wipes I found!" exclaimed Laura. "They are pretreated with a cleaning solution so you don't have to walk around with a roll of paper towels *and* a spray bottle. They are *all in one*!!"

I blinked. I was having déjà cleaning products.

As the cleaning wipes conversation continued I stood utterly speechless. Had I really left my cool life in New York City, moved to the burbs where I was surrounded by women who talked about cleaning products, struggled to find friends who talked about things besides cleaning products, reinvented myself, got my cool back, and then come to the city for a party where I was again thrown together with women who talked about cleaning products?

Apparently I had.

Realizing the irony, I started to giggle, and then snort, and then burst out laughing. The other women stopped talking and stared at me.

"I'm so sorry," I said, trying to turn the laugh into a cough. "I think a piece of chicken satay went down the wrong pipe." I coughed again. "Please excuse me!"

I ran from the group and found my husband talking to a bunch of people I didn't know.

"Ha-ha-ha! Cleaning products!" I sputtered, red in the face and laughing out loud.

"Honey, are you okay?"

"There were these other stay-at-home moms . . . and they . . . cleaning products . . ." I stammered, and then I burst out laughing again.

"This is my wife, Tracy," my husband said to the group. "I swear she only had one drink."

I made an effort to control myself and just as I said hello, I felt a tap on my shoulder. I turned and saw my former boss standing in front of me.

"Oh my God!" I bellowed. *"Jackson!!"*

With a huge grin on his face, all six-foot-two-ness of him enveloped me in a giant bear hug.

"I am so happy to see you here!" he exclaimed. "Never expected to see you here, but so happy you are."

I nodded. "Me, too!"

"How *are* you?" he wondered.

"I'm actually really good," I said.

"And how are the kids?"

"They're doing great!"

"I want to hear all about your life with the kids and how it's working out for you and for them," he said genuinely.

I stopped and stared.

"You do?"

"Absolutely!" he assured me.

I was floored. I was so sure this whole night would be about me trying to be scintillating without talking about my life as a stay-at-home mom, and yet here I had found someone from my former life who actually wanted to know about my life as a stay-at-home mom. There was no pretense or judgment about my worth based on what I did. Just honest-to-goodness interest and care.

"It may be a little boring," I admitted.

"That's okay," he said. "I left my job. I'm boring now, too. Come," he said, leading me to a table. "Let's bore each other!"

· · ·

"So, why did you leave?" I asked Jax as we nestled into a corner table with drinks. "I thought you'd be at the station until you died in that chair or were forced out."

"I was forced out," he replied, smiling.

"Oops," I said softly.

"No, it's fine," he said. "It was time, and the place had changed so much and my heart wasn't really in it anymore, anyway." He paused and took a sip from his drink. "It never got to the point where they actually asked me to leave. I just saw the writing on the wall and decided to go on my own terms."

"So where are you now?" I asked.

"Las Vegas."

"*What?* You left New York City?" I gasped. "I never thought you'd leave New York!"

"I never thought you'd leave New York, either." He laughed.

"Yeah, well, I was dragged kicking and screaming," I said. "Don't you miss the city?"

"Of course! There's no place like it."

"Clearly you haven't been to the suburbs," I remarked. "We have Walmart!"

"True. But we have Elvis," he stated.

"You left New York City for Elvis?"

"No, I left because my family is out there."

"Ah. Got it."

"How about you?" he asked. "How are you enjoying motherhood?"

"The motherhood part of it's been pretty good. You know, except for the five years when I was sleep-deprived, changing diapers, potty training, and buried under a mountain of laundry and Legos," I admitted.

He sighed. "I remember those days."

"It's getting easier now that the kids are in school. But truthfully, the tough part was giving up all the *me* stuff." I paused, wondering how much of this journey to divulge. Jax was my former boss, not my girlfriend. But he was someone who had known me really well "before," and I thought if anyone could understand the loss I had felt leaving my old life, it was him.

"I mean, I chose to do that," I continued. "I chose to leave my job and the city. But after I did, I was kind of lost, you know? I really had a lot invested in being the cool city chick with the cool TV job and when I didn't have that, I didn't seem to know who I was anymore. Does that make sense?"

"Yes. I get it. I know you loved your job and you were really good at it. And since we're being honest, I have to admit, when you quit, I wondered if you were going to be happy just being a mom," he said. "Which is not to say that *just* being a mom is a bad thing. But for you, I had a hunch you might feel like you needed more."

I inhaled deeply and felt my shoulders come down for what felt like the first time in eons.

"It wasn't just that I wasn't completely happy being home. I also felt really guilty that I wasn't completely happy being home, like somehow I was a failure as a mother because I wasn't completely fulfilled just spending time with my kids," I admitted.

"Sounds like it was a tough time," he said.

"You have no idea." I laughed.

"You seem like you're in a good place now, though," he observed.

"At some point I gave myself permission to say, 'I need more than just playdates and conversations about cleaning products to make me happy.' Then I started trying to figure out what that would look like, and now, I think, I really am happier. I also think I'm a better mother *because* I'm happier."

He smiled and took my hand.

"That sounded really dorky, didn't it?" I laughed.

"No," he said kindly. "I get it."

"Can I tell you something else?"

"What?"

"I was really nervous about coming to this party tonight. I felt like I had to prove that I was still cool and still relevant." I gestured to the other attendees, and as I looked around, I caught the eye of Garry scowling in our direction. "I thought that what these people thought of me would somehow affect how I felt about myself."

"Does that matter?" he asked, I realized, somewhat rhetorically.

I looked around at all the people I used to work with who were all trying hard to impress everyone else with how impressive they were and give the impression that they didn't care if anyone else was impressed or not. It seemed so transparent to me now. Why didn't I see it before? And if I did, why did I care?

"No," I said honestly. "It doesn't. Not anymore."

Chapter 21

Finding My Way Back to Cool

What is "cool," anyway? It might be difficult to define, but you know when you have it and you know when you've lost it.

I had thought cool was about my haircut and my clothes and the car I drove. But along the way of losing these things and then getting them back, I realized these were all just a reflection of the person I felt I was inside: someone who was unique, creative, and multidimensional. I loved being a mom, but I didn't want to look like a mom and only do mom things and only talk about mom stuff. Someday, probably sooner than I could imagine, my kids would be grown up and not need me in the same way that they did right now. When that day arrived, I wanted to feel that I had given them the very best of me I had to offer but hadn't lost that person in the process.

Truthfully, my kids didn't care what my hair looked like or what car we had, as long as it had a DVD player in it. They weren't going to remember if we had the latest tile in our bathroom or new kitchen cabinets. They were going to remember the vacations we took together with the money we didn't spend on new tiles or new cabinets, and the games we played together on the floor of their bedrooms, which were just the right size, not too big or too small, to accommodate us and all the various arms and legs of Mr. and Mrs. Potato Head. They didn't want a mom who spent all her time at the mall or playing tennis or hanging out with her decorator. They just wanted a mom who felt good about herself and felt good about being with them. Of course they didn't know this intellectually, but they knew the difference between a happy mommy and an unhappy one. If I needed some of those externals to feel good about myself, I don't think that was such a bad thing. As long as it wasn't the only thing I needed to feel good about myself. Ultimately that good feeling needed to come from within, but if fixing some of the outside helped me feel better on the inside so I could *get to a place* where it came from within, who's to say that was a bad road to take to get to where I wanted to be?

I was thinking about how far I had come one night as we all sat around the dinner table. While we ate, my daughter started telling us a story about a friend's mom who was not only gorgeous and thin but ran the PTA and did triathlons when she wasn't on missions in Mexico and Africa, and had single-handedly gotten the community to donate materials and labor to rebuild the home of a local family whose house had burned down and could not afford to rebuild it themselves.

I sat there picking at the food on my plate and suddenly felt significantly *less than*. Without realizing it, I let out a giant sigh.

"What's wrong, Mommy?" asked my daughter.

"Your friend's mom is thin and gorgeous and does important things like save the world. I am not thin and gorgeous and all I do is make peanut butter and jelly sandwiches and write funny columns." I blurted this out, undoing all the years of self-confidence building I had just achieved.

Emily just stared at me and then shook her head.

"Oh, Mommy, I think you are beautiful and what you do *is* important," she replied emphatically.

"You take care of us and your columns make people laugh. When people are sad or scared or feel bad, they read your columns and they feel better," she added. "That is the best thing ever."

My husband looked across the table and nodded at me.

I got it.

Later that night, I went upstairs with a renewed sense of well-being. I caught myself smiling as I thought about how ironic it was that I was learning about the kind of person I wanted to be from a five-year-old.

Somewhat nervously, I realized the real litmus test of how far I'd come was still ahead of me. As I began to lay out clothes for our upcoming beach vacation, I grabbed one of my bathing suits to see how it fit. While I squeezed into the tankini, consciously avoiding the full-length mirror, my daughter knocked on the door and came in.

"What do you think of this bathing suit?" she asked, modeling her own little tankini. She looked adorable in a little black-and-white polka-dotted swimsuit with a pink frilly bottom. Bathing suits with skirts on five-year-olds? Very cute. On thirty-six-year-olds? Not so much.

"What do *you* think?" I asked her back.

"I think I look *awesome!*" she boasted. I nodded in agreement.

"What do you think of mine?" I asked her, spinning around in my much larger swimsuit.

She stared thoughtfully at me.

"You have extra *butt* hanging out the back."

.   .   .

It's never easy to hear the truth about your butt, but if anyone is going to give it to you, it will most likely be a five-year-old. Fortunately, I was in a good place about my extra buttage— and my life in general—so the comment passed over me, rather than through me, somewhat painlessly. Still, I realized I probably needed to commit to that final ten-pound push to get to my pre-baby body weight, and I would definitely do that . . . just as soon as I had one more doughnut.

While I waited in line at the doughnut shop, I noticed the woman standing on line in front of me had a baby in an infant carrier over her arm and was holding the hands of two other kids under the age of five, trying to keep them far enough apart that they would stop trying to kill each other. She was dressed in a loose nursing shirt stained with something that appeared to formerly be food, had her hair pulled back in a scrunchie, and looked like she hadn't slept in a year. After placing her order, she looked at me and sighed.

"I used to be cool. Now I'm covered with drool."

"That was my motto for about five years." I laughed. "It gets better, I swear."

"Stop!" she suddenly barked at the little girl attached to her left hand who had desperately been trying to stomp on her brother's foot.

I jumped from the sudden outburst, which I had at first assumed was directed at me.

"You need a time-out. Go sit over there." She pointed to a corner next to the cold case. The little girl thrust out her lower lip but did as she was told.

"When?" she wondered, turning her attention back to me. "When does it get better?"

"Once they are all in school for at least a couple of hours a day, or as soon as you can sell them on eBay. I got a lot of money for mine," I assured her.

She grinned.

"Then you can use the time to work out or take a nap or get a tattoo," I continued.

"I'm dying to get a tattoo!" she exclaimed.

"I want a tattoo," said the little boy still clutching her other hand. He lifted up his sleeve and pointed to the place where his bulging bicep would be one day. "I want it here! And I want a motorcycle, too."

His mother snorted. "Yeah? Get in line!"

"Next!" announced the doughnut shop employee. I moved up to the counter and ordered my coffee.

"I used to be an attorney," said the mom. ". . . Before I quit to stay home and be the world's greatest mother."

"How's that working out?" I asked her.

"I was better at being an attorney," she admitted.

"What's an attorney?" asked her son.

She thought for a minute. "It's someone who defends good people and makes bad people go to jail."

"Oh, like a Power Ranger!" he said.

"Yeah, something like that."

"Are you going to go back to that one day?" I asked her.

"I don't think so," she sighed.

I nodded and we both waited in thoughtful silence for our orders.

"Okay, time-out is over," she announced to the little girl. Her daughter walked over and stuck her tongue out at her brother.

"What did I say you should do when you're angry at someone?" the mom asked the girl.

"Use your words, not your hands," the girl said dutifully.

". . . Or your feet," added the mom. "Right?" The girl nodded and then blew a big puff of air at her brother's face.

"Mommy!" whined the boy.

"How many kids do you have?" she asked, giving her daughter a death stare.

I nodded. "Two."

"Do you work?" she asked.

"Yes."

"What do you do?"

"I'm a full-time mom," I said confidently. "And I also write a humor column."

"Oh. That's a cool job!" She rotated her infant carrier and the two fidgeting kids so she could free a hand to collect her food and drinks.

"It sounds like you've been where I am but you figured it all out," she said as she headed to the door.

"Still trying to figure it all out," I admitted, racing over to get the door for her. "But certainly feeling a lot closer than I was six years ago!"

"What's the secret?" she wondered as she stopped and looked at me imploringly.

I thought for a minute. "First, I stopped defining myself

by what I 'used to be.' Instead, I thought about who I am now and who I wanted to be going forward. Second, I decided not to wait to be happy until my kids were older or I got it all figured out. I started doing things that made me happy now. Third—and I think this was the most important thing—I tried to look for the humor in the craziness and learn to laugh at it all. Once I started doing that, I really enjoyed being a mom so much more."

"Sounds like good advice. I think I'll try it," she said. "But it might need to wait a little while." She dropped one of her kids' hands and reached down to pat her stomach, revealing a bulge under the loose shirt. ". . . Until after number four!"

I gasped and she laughed.

"By the way," she shouted back to me as she left. "You have a really cool haircut."

*   *   *

Sometimes you don't realize something about yourself or your life until you say it out loud. That's what happened to me when I saw that other mom at the doughnut shop. Telling her the lessons I learned helped make it more real for me, and I suddenly realized I *was* enjoying my life more, I was happier, and I was truly finding the gifts in motherhood. This is not to say that everything was perfect. I still wasn't sure I had gotten my cool back, but I did feel like I had gotten in touch with a part of me I had lost when I quit my job and started popping out children.

I also realized, I never would actually be done trying to find my cool and never have everything exactly the way I wanted, because life with kids is constantly evolving. It doesn't stand still. The kids get older, the challenges change, and you realize it is a process . . . a journey. The flawless life I thought I had before I had kids was an illusion. The goal now was not to get it perfect, but to keep making my happiness, and the happiness of my family, the priority. To do this I had to maintain my individuality, because that was important to me, have an outlet for my creativity, and have like-minded friends to celebrate my joys with me and boost me up when things were tough. I needed a supportive family, a husband who helped me nurture my needs, and children who I could shower with love unconditionally and remind that they didn't need to be perfect, either. Most of all, I needed to be okay with everything sometimes being messy, because life is usually messy.

But it's also pretty cool.

Epilogue

~~~~~~~~~~

It had taken a long time, but I was finally feeling happy, secure, and settled in my new life . . . until I saw the flashing lights in my rearview mirror, once again.

I had just left the doughnut shop where I'd picked up a dozen doughnuts to bring to my playgroup with Lori, Shari, and Becca. No sooner had I turned the corner and headed up the main road than I heard the siren and noticed the telltale lights.

I cursed under my breath and quickly checked my speedometer to make sure I wasn't speeding. I wondered if maybe I had a taillight out or lost my license plate or had an expired registration, but I was fairly sure all my various car parts were in order. Finally, I checked to make sure I wasn't driving in my bathrobe.

Confident that I was a model citizen and excellent driver,

I eased the car over to the side of the road and waited an interminable amount of time for the police officer to get out of his vehicle and saunter over to me.

"License and registration, please," he said flatly.

I realized with a start that he was the same cop who busted me for driving in my bathrobe two years earlier. Clearly, the time had done nothing to improve his personality.

"Was I going too fast?" I inquired. "Too slow? Tailgating? Failure to yield to a pedestrian in a crosswalk?"

He ignored me and studied my license.

"Wait here," he said, and then walked back to his car. This was bad. I knew that he was going back to run my license and all of my minor suburban driving transgressions were going to appear.

Before I could ponder my fate, he suddenly reappeared. I looked at him expectantly.

He handed me back my license and grinned.

"You have a box of doughnuts on the roof of your car."

Acknowledgments

Where do I begin? There are so many of you who have been on this journey with me since the beginning, but I think first I need to thank all the little people who let me ignore them, push them out of my way, and forget to feed them in order to get this book written. (Sorry, kids. There's some leftover pizza in the fridge.)

To my amazing agent, Lynn, thank you for letting me accost you at someone else's book event and for agreeing to take on this project. I applaud your good taste and the fact that you always smiled when you told me to change something.

To my fabulous editor, Maria, I'm so glad you were seven months pregnant and about to move from the city to the suburbs when my proposal landed on your desk. That was the universe's gift to me for having endured prior rejections and also thirty-six hours of childbirth with my firstborn. And it was my gift to you for giving you something to *really* be worried about before you gave birth. To my editor, Jeanette, thanks for jumping in and helping guide me through the final stretch! And to all the other great folks at Perigee Books, thank you for your wonderful cover design, your amazing marketing ideas, and your ability to talk me down off the ledge.

To my publicist, Pam, who also had a baby while I was giving birth to this book, thank you for always being in my corner, even when your water was breaking. See, it's not as bad as I made it out to be. Okay, maybe a little. Don't say I didn't warn you about the hemorrhoids.

Thank you to my super-awesome mom friends who supported me through this process . . . Dana, Charlene, Michelle, Jennifer, Lisa, Randi, Lindsay, Wojo, my TV husband, Joe, and especially Bruce Cameron, who is not a mom but is in touch with his feminine side and sent me lots of funny, encouraging texts while he was out trying to promote his own books! Much gratitude as well to my incredibly supportive online mom community who are too many to name but I must give a special shout-out to Carissa, Jenny, Kristen, Nicole, Mary, Holly, Deb, and Anissa, and my dudes, Jim, Nick, and Matt. You have all been so much more than "virtual" friends. Thank you for your encouragement and for sharing your hilariously funny blogs that make me snort and gave me a wonderful place to go when I needed a break from my own writing. Thank you also to the Erma Bombeck Writers' Workshop, especially Teri and Matt, my *Balancing Act* family, my Erma Yahoo! group and the EB Heron girls, my Blogmitzvah gals, the awesome chicks at Aiming Low, and my National Society of Newspaper Columnists friends. You guys rock!

To my newspaper editors at the *Independent Press*, North Jersey Media Group, the *Mahopac News*, and GateHouse Media, especially Mike, Barbara, Carolyn, Joe, Brett, and Lisa, thank you for carrying my column all these years and being understanding when I still occasionally confuse "its" and "it's."

Thanks to Marsha and Victor, my legal sharks. Glad you're on *my* side!

Thanks to Vicki who had to listen to me talk incessantly about my book while she cut my hair . . . and she still gave me the world's best haircut!

Special thanks to my dear friend Ed, who ditched me in New Jersey to go play golf with alligators in Florida but always sent me lots of love and support between holes. Big thanks also to my friend Gordon Kirkland, who took me under his wing when I was just dipping my toe in the writing waters and let me spill wine on him and spit cheesecake on his tie without throwing me to the sharks. Gordon, you inspire me with your optimism, incredible sense of humor, and good taste in dinner partners.

Thanks to Lee, for letting me know when it was okay to let go of my old life and start my new one.

To my extended family, Harvey, Carol, Steve, Nancy, Rich, Paula, David, Emily, Wendy, Karen, Ken, and Jess, thanks for reading every column and blog, shouting from the rooftops on my behalf when I got this book deal, and not complaining too much when I wrote about you. Thanks also to Jordan, Sidney, Bela, Ady, Justin, Russell, and Cole for being the greatest bunch of nieces and nephews ever!

To my husband, Joel, words cannot begin to describe how much I love you and this wonderful journey we are on together. Thanks for being the love of my life, the father of my children, my partner, and my best friend. You are and will always be my Gilaman!

And to my children, Josh and Emily . . . You are my inspiration, the center of my universe, and the two very biggest blessings in my life. I am so grateful to have both of you, and I'm sorry for throwing out all your Happy Meal toys while you were away at camp. It was the only way.

About the Author

Tracy Beckerman writes the syndicated humor column and blog *Lost in Suburbia* (lostinsuburbia.com), which is carried by more than 400 newspapers in 25 states and on 250 related websites to approximately 10 million readers. She appears frequently on TV and radio and does stand-up comedy about how to be a cool mom in the suburbs. Yes, she knows that is an oxymoron. Tracy lives in the suburbs of New Jersey with her husband, two kids, and four goldfish named Larry. Follow her on Twitter @TracyinSuburbia.